Forgiving Day by Day

Practicing God's Ways in Our Relationships

Judith Ingram

Copyright © 2019 Judith Ingram

All rights reserved. No part of this publication may be reproduced or transmitted in any form or by any electronic or mechanical means including photo copying, recording, or any information storage and retrieval system now known or to be invented, without permission in writing from the publisher or the author.

ISBN: 978-1-945976-17-9

Scripture quotations noted CEB are taken from the Common English Bible, copyright © 2011. Used by permission. All rights reserved.

Scripture quotations marked ESV are from The Holy Bible, English Standard Version® (ESV®), copyright © 2001 by Crossway Bibles, a publishing ministry of Good News Publishers. Used by permission. All rights reserved.

Scripture quotations marked GNT are taken from the Good News Translation-Second Edition © 1992 by American Bible Society. Used by permission.

Scripture quotations marked MSG are taken from THE MESSAGE. Copyright © 1993, 1994, 1995, 1996, 2000, 2001, 2002. Used by permission of NavPress Publishing Group.

Scripture quotations marked NCV are from The Holy Bible, New Century Version®, copyright © 1987, 1988, 1991 by Word Publishing, a division of Thomas Nelson, Inc. Used by permission.

Scripture quotations marked NIV are taken from the Holy Bible, New International Version®, NIV®. Copyright © 1973, 1978, 1984, 2011 by Biblica, Inc.™ Used by permission. All rights reserved worldwide.

Scripture quotations marked NKJV are taken from the New King James Version, copyright © 1982 by Thomas Nelson, Inc. Used by permission. All rights reserved.

Scripture quotations marked NLT are taken from The Holy Bible, New Living Translation, copyright © 1996, 2004, 2007 by Tyndale House Foundation. Used by permission of Tyndale House Publishers, Inc., Carol Stream, Illinois 60188. All rights reserved.

Scripture quotations marked NRSV are from the New Revised Standard Version Bible, copyright © 1989 by the Division of Christian Education of the National Council of Churches of Christ in the U.S.A., and are used by permission. All rights reserved.

Filigree used by permission Free Vector Design by www.vecteezy.com

Published by EA Books Publishing, a division of
Living Parables of Central Florida, Inc. a 501c3

EABooksPublishing.com

For
Robert C. Richard, Ph.D.
who helped me find the path to forgiveness

Contents

Before You Begin 1

Week One 4
    Your Positive Pole 5
    Wounded Wounders 6
    Am I Sweet? 8
    Battle of the Grudge 9
    Defeating Evil 11
    Weekend Review 12

Week Two 14
    Winnowing the Chaff 15
    The Flawed Follower 16
    The First Stone 18
    Two Ears, One Mouth 20
    Resolutions That Stick 21
    Weekend Review 23

Week Three 26
    Hearts Toward God 27
    Lovely You 29
    My Brother's Keeper 30
    Firm Footing 32
    Why Not Gossip? 34
    Weekend Review 36

Week Four 38
    Kingdom Righteousness 39
    An Enduring Name 40
    Good Accounting 42

Forever Love 44

Circumcise Your Heart 45

Weekend Review 46

Week Five 48

Because We Are Dust 49

Rest Like a Child 50

Fill Up with God 52

Release from Regret 53

Choosing Sides 55

Weekend Review 56

Week Six 60

Reckoning Our Worth 61

God's Unstoppable Purpose 62

Recasting the Sinner 64

You Are My Witnesses 65

Living on the Edge 67

Weekend Review 68

Week Seven 72

The Danger in Blessings 73

Quality Faith 74

Blessed Gifting 76

Love Never Fails 77

Love Turned Bitter 79

Weekend Review 80

Week Eight 82

Looking for Grace 83

God Builds Us Up 84

Seeds for Sowing 85

>   Sinner or Saint?...87
>
>   Fruitful Prayer..89
>
>   *Weekend Review* 91

Week Nine...**94**

>   Born for Trouble 95
>
>   The Supernatural Power of Unity 96
>
>   Tenants for God 98
>
>   My True and Upright Self...99
>
>   The Best Revenge 101
>
>   *Weekend Review* 102

Week Ten **106**

>   Beauty from the Ashes..107
>
>   Eyes of Light..108
>
>   Go and Love 110
>
>   How to Get Even 111
>
>   Piety That Counts 113
>
>   *Weekend Review* 114

Week Eleven **118**

>   Fudging the Facts...119
>
>   Forgiver's Prayer..120
>
>   Asset or Stumbling Block? 122
>
>   How to Deflect Cruel Words 124
>
>   No Room for Idols 125
>
>   *Weekend Review* 127

Week Twelve **130**

>   Love Without Pause...131
>
>   Treasures of a Good Heart 132
>
>   Stinging Arrows 134

Living in Light 136

Sing a New Song 138

Weekend Review 139

A Blessing as You Go Out...**141**

About the Author..**142**

Before You Begin

Why this book?

Forgiveness is a holy practice every Christian needs for a vital and effective spiritual life. If we follow Christ as our Savior and trust the authority of the Bible, then we know that God calls us to forgive and make peace with one another, especially with our brothers and sisters in the faith. Forgiveness is an attribute of God that the Spirit also cultivates in us as we learn to live like Christ in our relationships. Even our common sense tells us we are better off when we let go of our negative baggage and seek peace with those who have injured us.

Despite all these good reasons to forgive, we still find that forgiving does not come easily. Particularly with our oldest and deepest wounds, we may believe that forgiving is impossible. We want to obey God and follow the ways of Christ, but injury has drawn a line we cannot cross. Thus trapped at the edge of our obedience, we cannot step ahead with God because pain and bitterness keep our attention fixed on the past.

This spiritual edge has been called a desert or a wilderness place, where God meets us and helps us to cross over. This book of devotionals is meant to be a handbook for such desert times with God.

How to use this book

The book is a collection of devotionals that focus on what Scripture has to say about living God's way in our relationships. It features twelve weeks of meditations and reflective exercises structured for your daily use.

Weekday Devotionals. Each devotional begins with Scripture and develops discussion on a topic that can help you learn and practice healthier relationships with God, yourself, and other people. Each devotional closes with a prayer and prompts for reflection and further reading, along with a simple takeaway statement.

Weekend Review. After five days of daily devotionals, the weekend offers you a chance to pause and reflect on your experience. Structured in six sequential steps, the weekend exercise is a variation of the Examen, a spiritual practice developed by Saint Ignatius of Loyola in the sixteenth century. The weekend review helps you look for God's presence and activity in your life as you read each devotional, pondered new insights, and put them into practice. It offers additional time to spend with God, listening for spiritual guidance and resting in God's care before heading into the next week of devotionals. Each weekend review closes with the prayer of a church mother or father as a final word of encouragement.

Resources you'll need

Access to Scripture. God speaks to us through Scripture, so you'll want to be ready to receive whatever God has for you. Use whichever Bible translation makes the most sense to you. A study Bible with commentary is helpful but not necessary. You can easily access Scripture with online Bible resources such as www.biblegateway.com and www.blueletterbible.org.

Journal. A journal is helpful for writing your answers to reflection questions and jotting down notes and insights you receive. Consider your journaling a time of prayer, for God may speak with you as you write and reflect.

Quiet time and space. Your twelve-week journey will work best if you can set aside daily time and a quiet space where you will not be interrupted. Making these devotions a fixed part of your daily routine will help you to think about forgiveness more often and practice forgiveness more naturally in your daily life.

Commitment. Before you read the first word of the first devotional, talk with God about your commitment. Decide whether you are willing to set aside time every day to listen for what God has to teach you. Determine whether you will keep going to the end, despite any resistance you may encounter. God promises to meet you in that desert place and give you exactly what you need to cross over. Let God help you on your journey.

My prayer for you

Heavenly Father, receive this pilgrim, who is on a journey to seek your heart and your will for (his/her) relationships. Grant this pilgrim the grace and comfort of your presence and the reassurance that (he/she) does not travel this road alone. Teach through your holy Word; counsel through the wisdom of your Spirit. As need arises, gently confront and guide this pilgrim to confession, repentance, and new resolve.

Where there is hardness of heart, soften. Where there is deep pain and suffering, comfort and heal. Where there is brokenness, mend and restore to wholeness. Give generously of your strength when the journey gets rough, and courage to keep going. Surround this precious child with your angels, deflecting all lies and schemes of your adversary, the devil, who is bent on defeating this holy quest. May this pilgrim find peace and hope in your promise that whoever diligently seeks you will find you (Proverbs 8:17).

It is in the powerful and compassionate Name of Jesus that I offer this prayer. Amen.

Week One

Monday

Your Positive Pole

Looking at his disciples, he said…"But to you who are listening I say: Love your enemies, do good to those who hate you, bless those who curse you, pray for those who mistreat you. If someone slaps you on one cheek, turn to them the other also. If someone takes your coat, do not withhold your shirt from them. Give to everyone who asks you, and if anyone takes what belongs to you, do not demand it back. Do to others as you would have them do to you." (Luke 6:20, 27-31 NIV)

Have you ever tried to push together the negative poles of two magnets? They repel each other, and the more you try to force them together, the stronger they resist connection. Short of an overriding external force, the only way those two magnets will come together is if one of them flips its position and approaches the other with its positive pole.

Relationships can be like that. When we are in the throes of conflict, approaching each other with our negative poles only increases our resistance to each other. For example, if you and I are both angry and defensive over an incident, the more we engage each other through our negativity, the more likely we are to resist connection and reinforce the strength of our negative positions.

Jesus summed up these polarity problems in the passage quoted above. He begins his discourse by saying, in effect, "To those of you who are willing to work at resolving conflict and healing your relationships, I have the solution for you." He then proceeds with a command that runs contrary to our natural inclinations. He says to respond with goodness and mercy to the evil that is done to us.

He lists some evils—enmity, hatred, cursing, maltreatment, injury, insult, theft—as negative poles that naturally provoke negative responses in us. Instead, he says, surprise your enemy by flipping your polarity and responding with positivity. Offer your enemy your positive pole—love, goodness, kindness, blessing, prayers on the other's behalf, humility, vulnerability, generosity—to demonstrate that your desire to reestablish a connection is more important to you than winning an argument or holding out for a just outcome.

Heavenly Father, I confess I am all too ready to respond to an insult or offense with my negative pole. Indignation, self-righteous posturing, and resentment seem to leap into position without my conscious volition. Help me to recognize when I am approaching an adversary with my negative pole, and help me flip my position. Thank you that you always respond to my negativity with goodness and mercy that I do not deserve. May I follow your example and offer those healing graces to those who oppose and mistreat me. Amen.

Dig Deeper: Romans 7:23-25; 12:21

Reflect: What kind of mistreatment is most likely to provoke a negative response from me? If I could reverse my polarity, what might my positive response look like?

Thought for Today: Surprise your enemy with loving kindness.

Tuesday

Wounded Wounders

> This is what the LORD says: Be fair-minded and just. Do what is right! Help those who have been robbed; rescue them from their oppressors. Quit your evil deeds! Do not mistreat foreigners, orphans, and widows. Stop murdering the innocent! (Jeremiah 22:3 NLT)

Through his prophet Jeremiah, God describes his social policy for right living among his people. The theme is familiar and repeated throughout the Old and New Testaments: Be just, righteous, and merciful. Be ready to help those who need your help and never be the one to add to another's misery.

If you are having difficulty with the idea of forgiving someone who has hurt you, you might try recasting your situation in the terms God describes. Consider how your offender might be viewed as one who has been "robbed" or "oppressed," and you as the one who can help him or her.

Different Bible translations offer alternative descriptions for the one who has been "robbed," such as the spoiled, the wronged, the victim of exploiters, the cheated, and the plundered. Likewise, the "oppressor" can be translated as the one who robs, attacks, exploits, cheats, extorts, or makes false accusations.

Does this oppressor sound familiar?

The apostle Peter describes this oppressor as "your enemy the devil" who "prowls around like a roaring lion looking for someone to devour" (1 Peter 5:8 NLT). Scripture depicts this enemy elsewhere as the accuser, lying spirit, tempter, prince of demons, and spirit that works in the children of disobedience. Every person born on this earth is prey to this cunning and merciless adversary. No one escapes the damage that evil perpetrates. We all bear scars from our own sin as well as from the hurtful acts of others, sometimes breaking or crippling us in ways that make healthy relationships difficult or impossible.

We can't know what makes people act the way they do. Unlike God, we can't see into their hearts to determine motives; we don't know all the life experiences that have shaped their character and taught them how to deal with others. Our idea of justice may shift when we consider how those who offend us may themselves have been robbed, cheated, exploited, or "spoiled." How might their concept of love or goodness have been twisted, or their dignity or innocence taken from them? How might their hope have been stolen and replaced with fear, hatred, or desperation?

When facing that person we cannot forgive, we can choose whether to respond as just one more oppressor or to allow compassion to temper us. With God's help, we might offer mercy instead and the hope of Christ, who bears the only Name in the universe that can take on the evil of this world and win.

Heavenly Father, it's difficult for me to feel compassion and mercy toward someone who has been cruel. However, because you require justice and righteousness from me, I ask for grace and courage to obey. Help me to recast people who wound and offend me so that I can see them as prey to the evil influences of a world under Satan's rule. Keep me from adding to their misery with punishing or vengeful acts of my own. Instead, let me be a help and a light for the sake of your kingdom. Amen

Dig Deeper: Isaiah 58:6-9; Zechariah 7:8-9; James 2:12-13

Reflect: In what way has the evil of this world stolen something from me? How has this loss affected me?

Thought for Today: God calls us to help and protect the very people who injure us.

Wednesday

Am I Sweet?

Taste and see that the LORD is good. (Psalm 34:8 NIV)

What tastes better than a basket of sweet summer strawberries or cherries picked right off the tree? The fragrance of a sun-warmed peach can make our mouths water; the sweetness of a plump, juicy grape invites us to sample another, and another.

It seems no coincidence that God chose *fruit* as a metaphor for the work of the Holy Spirit in us. When I bring love and goodness and kindness and gentleness into my relationships, others taste the sweetness of God. Our Father gives us this good fruit for the benefit and nourishment of those around us. Indeed, as priests of our King, we have the honor and responsibility to bring the goodness of God's kingdom into every circumstance and relationship we encounter.

The next time you are tempted to respond to an offense with harsh words or hurtful retaliation, ask yourself, *what taste of God and his kingdom will my actions bring to this person—sweet or bitter?*

Heavenly Father, thank you for your sweet goodness. Help me to remember that as a royal priest and a member of your family, I am entrusted with helping others learn more about you. Please take the bitterness out of my "fruit" and make my actions sweet and wholesome for the nourishment of others, even my adversaries. Amen

Dig Deeper: Song of Songs 2:3; Galatians 5:22-23; 1 Peter 2:9

Reflect: When has being forgiven brought sweetness into my life?

Thought for Today: The sweetness of forgiveness gives people a taste of God's goodness.

Thursday

Battle of the Grudge

> The sinful nature wants to do evil, which is just the opposite of what the Spirit wants. And the Spirit gives us desires that are the opposite of what the sinful nature desires. These two forces are constantly fighting each other, so you are not free to carry out your good intentions. (Galatians 5:17 NLT)

Our sinful nature is always willing to do battle over injuries and insults we suffer in relationships. Selfish motives compel us to hurt back, punish, or escalate conflict rather than to let some wrongdoer off the hook. Far from wanting to appear weak, we may even argue our moral obligation to teach the wrongdoer a lesson for the good of humanity.

Paul calls this kind of thinking slavery to our sin nature. The Spirit, he claims, has come to set us free, not so we can indulge our natural inclinations but so we can love and serve God by loving and serving one another.

Faith teaches us that we have nothing to fear from our neighbors. We can afford to be generous and forgiving because our souls are safe and our value is guaranteed through the saving grace of Christ's death for us on the cross. What truly threatens us is the evil that tempts us away from God and leads us into quarrels and jealousy and vengeful behavior.

Although God desires that we forgive one another, our pain over an injury may be so great that forgiving seems utterly impossible. If that's true for you, take heart and don't try to force the issue.

Instead, offer a simple prayer: "Father, give me faith to love you more."

Just that. Pray it several times a day. Pray it every day. If you do, two things will happen:

- God will honor your prayer and give you what you ask. God will fill you with the reassurance of his Spirit because that's what he desires and has promised to do.

- God's Spirit will form in you desires that your sinful nature will resist but cannot defeat—desires to love and be merciful and in every way manifest your Father's loving nature in your life and your relationships.

Heavenly Father, give me faith to love you more. Amen

Dig Deeper: Ephesians 2:8-10; Galatians 5:13-15

Reflect: How can love for God help me let go of a grudge?

Thought for Today: We can afford to forgive because our souls are safe and our worth is secure.

Friday

Defeating Evil

Every child of God defeats this evil world, and we achieve this victory through our faith. And who can win this battle against the world? Only those who believe that Jesus is the Son of God. (1 John 5:4-5 NLT)

When trouble comes at us through a relationship, it helps to remember that we are part of an ongoing spiritual battle. Satan is at war with God, and part of his strategy to defeat God is to hurt God's children.

The pain we suffer in human conflict may drive us away from God, or it can lead us closer if we ask, *what is the evil in this situation that I need God to help me overcome?*

- Am I being threatened with harm?
- Do I feel tempted to sin?
- Is my faith as a follower of Christ being shaken?
- Am I falling prey to self-doubt or to guilt and remorse over things I have done?
- Are my flaws and fears being exploited?

We cannot escape this great spiritual battle, but our faith and trust in God can help us deal with it. The Spirit can teach us how to identify and oppose the evil in a conflict without our hating and opposing the other person, whom God dearly loves and for whom Jesus died.

Our Savior assures us that he has overcome every evil that we face in this world. Moreover, he promises that we, too, can defeat evil if we put our hope and trust in him.

Heavenly Father, I have been shocked and hurt by the evil that has come at me through my relationships. Give me faith to stand strong in your work of salvation on the cross, where you defeated all that assaults me now. I ask for wisdom to see my true adversary in Satan and not in other humans who, like me, are susceptible to being used for evil purposes. Thank you that evil will not have the last word in my life as I daily choose to follow you. Amen

Dig Deeper: John 16:33; 1 John 4:4

Reflect: What weakness in me is Satan most likely to exploit through human conflict?

Thought for Today: When we belong to Christ, evil will never have the last word.

Saturday/Sunday

Weekend Review

Settle in: I quiet myself and acknowledge God's presence. I offer God my time and attention. I ask the Spirit to help me review my week with clarity and understanding.

Review with gratitude: I allow memories of the week to flow through me like a slow river. I notice special moments and gifts, large and small, for which I am thankful. I take some time to acknowledge these blessings before God and express my gratitude.

Celebrate: I recall what went well for me this week.

- When did I experience life-giving feelings, such as joy, peace, love, generosity, or being on a right path?
- When did I feel God's nearness?
- How did I practice new insights from my forgiveness work this week?
- In what ways did God counsel and help me this week?

Confront: I recall what did not go well for me this week.

- When did I experience life-draining feelings, such as anger, anxiety, envy, sadness, fear, rebelliousness, or being on a wrong path?

- When did God seem most distant?

- What forgiveness practices did I find difficult or impossible?

- In what ways did I resist God's counsel and help this week?

Talk it over: I talk with God about what I've discovered.

- I praise and thank God for the work of his Spirit in my life this week.

- I acknowledge areas of my life where I am resistant to God's call and counsel.

- I ask God for the grace I need to continue this journey of forgiving and practicing God's ways in my relationships.

Close with prayer: I pray along with this prayer of Origen (c. 185-254):

Jesus, my feet are dirty. Come even as a slave to me, pour water into your bowl, come and wash my feet. In asking such a thing I know I am overbold, but I dread what was threatened when you said to me, "If I do not wash your feet I have no fellowship with you." Wash my feet then, because I long for your companionship. Amen

Week Two

Monday

Winnowing the Chaff

> But when he saw many of the Pharisees and Sadducees coming to where he was baptizing, he said…"I baptize you with water for repentance. But after me comes one who is more powerful than I, whose sandals I am not worthy to carry. He will baptize you with the Holy Spirit and fire. His winnowing fork is in his hand, and he will clear his threshing floor, gathering his wheat into the barn and burning up the chaff with unquenchable fire." (Matthew 3:7, 11-12 NIV)

To the farmers of Jesus' time, *winnowing* (or threshing) was a familiar harvest event. A winnowing fork was used to toss ripe grain into the air so that the wind could blow away the worthless chaff, preserving the valuable kernels. In the above passage, John the Baptizer uses winnowing as an analogy for God's judgment, when the righteous will be separated from the unrighteous and saved. We can further use the image of winnowing to help us understand how forgiveness works.

When we first sustain a personal injury, a crowd of emotions can flood our hearts: anger, surprise, disappointment, indignation, sorrow, or fear. Given time, these emotions can harden into resentment and bitterness. We nurse grudges and entertain fantasies of revenge. We may rehearse stories to tell others about how we have suffered unjustly. Sometimes we cover our emotions with a blanket of indifference, convincing ourselves that the injury did not matter.

All these hardened responses to injury are as worthless and lifeless as the chaff that encases the valuable heart of a grain. Yet we cling to them with the idea that we need them. We use them as barriers to protect ourselves from further injury or to punish the wrongdoer. Encasing our hearts in resentment may become so habitual that we don't even realize we have a choice.

In choosing to forgive, we surrender our injured hearts to the Holy Spirit, who blows through us like a cleansing wind, discarding the worthless chaff and preserving what is precious. Through the healing work of God's love and nurturing presence, we come to realize what truly matters in life and let go of what does not. Winnowing the chaff releases us from its grip and frees us to rebuild a damaged relationship.

Heavenly Father, I confess that the chaff surrounding my injured heart can be so attractive that I cannot imagine giving it up. I ask for the courage to surrender my heart to the purging power of your Spirit Wind. Help me to recognize the worthless, lifeless nature of my resentment and to desire instead the freedom that comes from forgiving others. Amen

Dig Deeper: Matthew 5:44; John 3:8

Reflect: How have I encased my heart in worthless chaff?

Thought for Today: When we forgive, God's Spirit blows through us like a cleansing wind.

Tuesday

The Flawed Follower

> So the soldiers, their commanding officer, and the Temple guards arrested Jesus and tied him up....Simon Peter followed Jesus, as did another of the disciples. That other disciple was acquainted with the high priest, so he was allowed to enter the high priest's courtyard with Jesus. Peter had to stay outside the gate. Then the disciple who knew the high priest spoke to the woman watching at the gate, and she let Peter in. (John 18:12, 15-16 NLT)

We all know what happens next. When challenged about his acquaintance with Jesus, Peter denies knowing him, not once but three times. Focusing on this failure of loyalty, however, we tend to overlook the love and loyalty that compelled Peter to follow Jesus in the first place.

Peter and the other disciple (probably John) certainly risked arrest themselves by following Jesus into the gated and guarded courtyard of the high priest. This high priest was so angry and jealous of Jesus that he was willing to condemn Jesus on false testimony and convince Rome to execute him. There is no doubt such wrath would have extended to Jesus' followers as well.

Peter, the disciple who got out of the boat during a storm to walk on water toward Jesus, did not lack courage. Nor did he lack faith, as he was the first to declare that Jesus was the expected Messiah. In the aftershock of seeing his beloved Master arrested, Peter succumbed to human frailty and fear. He doubted what he knew about Jesus. He forgot Jesus' promises and miracles. He did not fully understand all that being a follower of Jesus must mean.

Perhaps most significant for us, Peter had not yet witnessed Jesus' sacrifice and resurrection, so he did not share our advantage of historical hindsight. He felt abandoned, disillusioned, and shaken.

Years later, the older and experienced apostle would encourage Christians to build their faith and hope in God through the practice of following Jesus: "Through Christ you have come to trust in God. And you have placed your faith and hope in God because he raised Christ from the dead and gave him great glory" (1 Peter 1:21 NLT).

Like Peter, we follow Christ with imperfect faith and hearts of divided loyalties, yet we follow. We make wrong decisions, we act selfishly and foolishly, yet we follow. We follow as Peter followed, because we love Jesus and know that our only hope lies in our Lord's love for us. Peter spoke for each of us when he told Jesus, "Lord, to whom would we go? You have the words of eternal life. We believe, and we know you are the Holy One of God" (John 6:68-69 NLT).

Heavenly Father, I offer you my imperfect faith and my heart pulled in so many directions as the world tempts and distracts me. Forgive me, as you forgave Peter, for stumbling in my efforts to follow you. Thank you for your love that never wavers and never condemns me but lifts me to where you are. Amen

Dig Deeper: John 10:27-30; 1 Peter 1:23

Reflect: Instead of dwelling on my failures, I can think of ways I have chosen to follow Jesus during the past week.

Thought for Today: Discipleship means following Jesus not faultlessly but faithfully.

Wednesday

The First Stone

The scribes and the Pharisees brought a woman who had been caught in adultery; and making her stand before all of them, they said to him, "Teacher, this woman was caught in the very act of committing adultery. Now in the law Moses commanded us to stone such women. Now what do you say?" They said this to test him, so that they might have some charge to bring against him. Jesus bent down and wrote with his finger on the ground. When they kept on questioning him, he straightened up and said to them, "Let anyone among you who is without sin be the first to throw a stone at her." And once again he bent down and wrote on the ground. (John 8:3-7 NRSV)

When we are faced with someone's moral transgression, as was Jesus in the above story, we must weigh together justice and mercy. Both must be considered for the good of the individual who stands accused as well as for the good of the community. Over time the religious leaders of Jesus' day had placed increasing emphasis on justice at the expense of mercy. In this story, Jesus reasserts the heart of the law by drawing on compassion from the crowd.

The Latin root for the word *compassion* means to bear with or to suffer with another person. Compassion allows us to enter into another person's distress and, even further, to be moved to alleviate that distress. We feel *with* rather than *against* the other person. We feel moved to help rather than to condemn.

In one simple statement, Jesus exposes the hypocrisy of the accusing crowd and makes a case for compassion. Who among you, he says in effect, is so pure and above reproach that you can find no common ground with this woman's moral failure? Who can look at this woman and not see your own shame and guilt mirrored? Who can stand before God on your own merit as one who does not need rescue from the traps and guiles of sin?

Scripture shows us the effects of Jesus' words in the next verse: "When they heard it, they went away, one by one, beginning with the elders; and Jesus was left alone with the woman standing before him" (v. 8).

Who were the first to feel convicted by Jesus' statement? They were the elders, the religious leaders in the crowd, the teachers who knew the law of Moses better than anyone. It seems a little astonishing that not one of them picked up a stone and threw it at the woman just to save face. Scripture tells us that each of the elders backed off, and the younger ones followed until the woman was left alone with Jesus.

What are the stones that you like to throw at "sinners" in your life? Are they words of accusation or insult, of reproach or gossip? Do you fling rejection or a cold shoulder at the person who offends you? Do you punish with silence that elevates you to a position of moral superiority?

Before you throw the next stone, ask yourself the same questions that Jesus put to the woman's accusers. Allow the Spirit to expose your weakness, not to condemn you but to show you the sin that makes you just like the other sinners in your life. Only then might you enter into their distress with them and be moved to find ways to help and heal their suffering.

Heavenly Father, expose my arrogance that leads me to judge others from a superior position. Remind me of my sin in those circumstances when I am tempted to condemn others. Take the stone from my hand and give me grace to forgive those who hurt and offend me. Amen

Dig Deeper: Romans 3:23; Colossians 3:13

Reflect: When have I been hit by someone's stone of condemnation? What form did that stone take? Have I ever thrown that same kind of stone myself?

Thought for Today: Admitting we are all sinners can move us from condemnation to compassion.

Thursday

Two Ears, One Mouth

To answer before listening—that is folly and shame. (Proverbs 18:13 NIV)

It's been said that God gave each of us two ears but only one mouth for good reason: talking-plus-talking-minus-listening-equals-conflict. Imagine how many novels would be left unwritten if on the first page the characters would just sit down and listen to each other. If there's no conflict, there's no story.

James 1:19 tells us we should be quick to listen but slow to speak. That's because understanding comes only through listening and allowing ourselves to be moved by what the other person has to say. When we stop talking and truly listen, we risk learning something that may change us intellectually and emotionally.

Intellectual risk – We may have to rethink our position or admit we were wrong. We may be persuaded to do something we do not want to do, or give up something that we prize.

Emotional risk – We may be forced to unblock feelings of compassion or grief or guilt. We may have to deal with anger, whether ours or the other person's. We may feel the relationship shifting us into new roles and unfamiliar ways of relating to each other.

Listening is an art and a skill that's worth cultivating. When we're talking, we're not listening, and we're putting the burden of understanding on the other person. The Bible tells us to be quick to take that burden of understanding onto ourselves and be slow to lay it on the other person's shoulders.

Heavenly Father, I confess I could do a better job of listening. Teach me this skill and help me to take on the burden of understanding more often. Amen

Dig Deeper: Psalm 81:11-12; James 1:19

Reflect: With whom in my life could I do a better job of listening?

Thought for Today: To listen is to risk being moved by another's words.

Friday

Resolutions That Stick

Throw off your old sinful nature and your former way of life, which is corrupted by lust and deception. Instead, let the Spirit renew your thoughts and attitudes. Put on your new nature, created to be like God—truly righteous and holy. (Ephesians 4:22-24 NLT)

"Headaches are like resolutions. You forget them as soon as they stop hurting."

This quote from the movie *Psycho* (1960) gives us a clue as to why our New Year's resolutions tend to give out before the winter snow melts. We may think we want to lose weight, give up smoking, or save more money, but unless the motivating hurt runs deep, we probably won't change our ways. Our old, familiar habits have too firm a grip on us.

In the Ephesians passage above, Paul describes the motivating hurt for Christians who want to change their ways. We hurt because we are not who we were created to be, which is the perfect reflection of God's own image. We live with a powerful sin nature that drives us to do things we know are not good for us, that offend the people around us and keep us distant from God. "Lust and deception"—that is, thirst for pleasure and willingness to lie and cheat to get what we want—damage our relationships and erode our self-respect.

When the Spirit convicts us, our hurt runs deep. We realize the ugliness of our sinful ways and how far we have fallen from the shining beings God created us to be. We gaze upon God, we see his goodness and light and love, and we understand how our resolutions are hopelessly inadequate for making us "like God—truly righteous and holy." We need God's grace and forgiveness to make us right.

Our best help for changing our ways is to give the Spirit full access to our minds and hearts. We must accept the hurt of realizing our sinful ways and let that pain motivate us to surrender our thoughts and attitudes to the Spirit, who promises to cleanse and restore us.

Heavenly Father, I give you my heart and my life. Show me all the ways I have strayed from being the person you created me to be. Help me not to fear the pain of exposure but to allow that pain to motivate change in me. I believe that no matter what I've done with my life or how I have sinned, what you originally created in me remains intact—fine and beautiful and uncorrupted. Restore me, Holy Spirit, to that perfect reflection of you. Amen

Dig Deeper: Romans 12:1-2; Psalm 51

Reflect: Why is pain such an effective motivator for change?

Thought for Today: The pain of acknowledging our sin motivates us to change.

Saturday/Sunday

Weekend Review

Settle in: I quiet myself and acknowledge God's presence. I offer God my time and attention. I ask the Spirit to help me review my week with clarity and understanding.

Review with gratitude: I allow memories of the week to flow through me like a slow river. I notice special moments and gifts, large and small, for which I am thankful. I take some time to acknowledge these blessings before God and express my gratitude.

Celebrate: I recall what went well for me this week.

- When did I experience life-giving feelings, such as joy, peace, love, generosity, or being on a right path?
- When did I feel God's nearness?
- How did I practice new insights from my forgiveness work this week?
- In what ways did God counsel and help me this week?

Confront: I recall what did not go well for me this week.

- When did I experience life-draining feelings, such as anger, anxiety, envy, sadness, fear, rebelliousness, or being on a wrong path?
- When did God seem most distant?
- What forgiveness practices did I find difficult or impossible?
- In what ways did I resist God's counsel and help this week?

Talk it over: I talk with God about what I've discovered.

- I praise and thank God for the work of his Spirit in my life this week.

Week Two

- I acknowledge areas of my life where I am resistant to God's call and counsel.
- I ask God for the grace I need to continue this journey of forgiving and practicing God's ways in my relationships.

Close with prayer: I pray along with this Prayer of Confession #3, from the *Book of Common Worship*:

Gracious God,

our sins are too heavy to carry,

too real to hide,

and too deep to undo.

Forgive what our lips tremble to name,

what our hearts can no longer bear,

and what has become for us

a consuming fire of judgment.

Set us free from a past that we cannot change;

open to us a future in which we can be changed;

and grant us grace

to grow more and more in your likeness and image;

through Jesus Christ, the light of the world. Amen

Week Three

Monday

Hearts Toward God

Be careful then, dear brothers and sisters. Make sure that your own hearts are not evil and unbelieving, turning you away from the living God....For if we are faithful to the end, trusting God just as firmly as when we first believed, we will share in all that belongs to Christ. (Hebrews 3:12, 14 NLT)

It's a package deal: Choosing to follow Christ not only rescues us from God's judgment but also commits our lives to God's lordship. From the moment we surrender, our daily challenges become testing grounds for our character as the Spirit works with us to make us more and more like our Savior.

Practically speaking, our initial decision to give our lives to God is only the first in a long series of turning-point decisions. With each new situation that arises, we must ask ourselves whether we will seek God's desire first or pursue our own agenda, whether we will follow in Christ's footsteps or not.

For example, if I am struggling in a relationship dilemma, I can stop wringing my hands or clenching my fists, and instead ask myself, *what would it mean for me to turn my heart toward God right now, in this moment?* Such a decision might lead me to take action in a way I would not otherwise consider:

- Seeing good in the other person instead of only what offends me.

- Dropping the label "adversary" or "offender" to describe the other person.

- Choosing to forgive.

- Facing an unpleasant truth about myself.

- Initiating a bold, positive move and trusting God to help me carry it through.

- Facing the reality that the relationship may never be what I'd hoped for.
- Making a difficult but necessary decision that I have been avoiding.
- Giving up control and asking God for my next step.
- Offering an apology.
- Working to change a selfish attitude or behavior in myself.

In turning my heart toward God, I release the situation to God and to the outcome that he has planned. My desires can take a backseat to God's agenda because I trust that he has my ultimate good in mind. God also rewards my obedience with the benefit of sharing "in all that belongs to Christ." I can enjoy the friendship of Christ as my sovereign Lord, elder brother, sympathetic advocate before the Father, and trustworthy Shepherd who always leads me in the right path.

Heavenly Father, I confess to many times when I have felt stuck in a relationship conflict and yet have resisted giving you lordship over the situation. At such times, nudge my heart to turn toward you. Reshape my attitudes to reflect your heart and guide my actions to serve your plan. Thank you for sending your Word and your Spirit to direct my steps. Amen

Dig Deeper: Joshua 24:15; Psalm 119:14; John 5:19

Reflect: How might turning my heart toward God change a relationship conflict in my life right now?

Thought for Today: God bathes our hearts in grace when we turn toward him.

Tuesday

Lovely You

How lovely is your dwelling place, O LORD of Heaven's Armies. (Psalm 84:1 NLT)

When the psalmist wrote this song, he was far away from the temple in Jerusalem. Although he wrote with longing for the courts of the Lord, it was not the temple building that drew him but rather the Lord who dwelt there. How lovely, the poet sang, to be in the presence of God, who loves his people so much that he makes his home in their midst.

Because of Jesus, God's temple has moved from a building in Jerusalem into the hearts and lives of the people who call themselves the Church. Each of us who follows Jesus has become the dwelling place of God's holy and eternal Spirit. Taking our cue from the psalmist, we might ask ourselves, *how lovely is God's dwelling place in me?*

We might condemn ourselves for all that is unlovely in our lives. Yet we must remember that God chooses to make his home in us despite our weaknesses and sin. God calls us with merciful love and then, at our yielding, sends his Spirit to cleanse, refine, and transform us into a holy people—righteous because of Jesus, hopeful because we are promised eternal life with God, and *lovely* because God lives in us. The more space in our lives we yield to God's power and will, the more we will shine with God's loveliness.

God infuses us with divine grace and goodness and then sets us as beacons to shine his loveliness into our relationships. With gracious words and loving acts, we become the lovely dwelling of God in the midst of our families and neighborhoods, schools and businesses. Through our transparency and faith, people who suffer from the ugliness of a selfish and hurtful world may recognize their need for the peace and beauty only God can offer and open their hearts to God's redeeming hope.

Heavenly Father, I am thankful for your loving Spirit that chooses to dwell in me. Show me the unlovely thoughts and attitudes in my life that keep people from seeing your true beauty. Teach me to yield more of my life to you, that my words may refresh and heal and my actions bring people closer to you. Amen

Dig Deeper: John 1:14; 1 Corinthians 3:16

Reflect: Who in my life needs to see God's loveliness in me?

Thought for Today: God's holy presence in our lives makes us lovely.

Wednesday

My Brother's Keeper

Cain said to his brother Abel, "Let us go out to the field." And when they were in the field, Cain rose up against his brother Abel, and killed him. Then the LORD said to Cain, "Where is your brother Abel?" He said, "I do not know; am I my brother's keeper?" (Genesis 4:8-9 NRSV)

When God questions Cain about his actions, Cain gives a classic denial of accountability. *The Message* translation captures the sarcasm: "How should I know? Am I his babysitter?"

In his flippant response, Cain nevertheless raises a serious question for which we need an answer: *How responsible am I for another person's welfare? For what does God hold me personally accountable?*

The Hebrew word for "keeper" in this verse is the same used to describe God in Psalm 121. The song names God as the divine One who keeps Israel, who guards and protects the body, mind, heart, and daily life of his people. As God's ambassadors for his kingdom on earth, we too have responsibilities in guarding and protecting the welfare of others.

According to Scripture, we are accountable for "keeping" one another in several ways:

- We forgive and love our offenders, thus relieving them of a burden that could crush their spirit (2 Corinthians 2:5-8).

- We help and encourage one another (Ecclesiastes 4:9-12; Romans 15:1-2).

- We show mercy and compassion to those in distress (Luke 10:25-37).

- We pray for each other (Matthew 5:44; James 5:16).

- We go and reconcile with those who have something against us (Matthew 5:24).

- We take care not to be a stumbling block to the weak (1 Corinthians 8:9).

- We rebuke sin that is harming another's spiritual walk (Proverbs 27:5-6).

- We denounce false teachings that hurt and cause division among God's people (1 Timothy 4:6-7; Jude 17-23).

To summarize, we are to watch over one another and be a resource of love, help, protection, and encouragement, not only to our friends and fellow believers but to our enemies as well.

Noticeably absent from our list of accountabilities is the other person's response. In reality, when we offer forgiveness, our offender may still refuse to reconcile. Even though we expose sin and false teaching, our loved one may continue down a dark path. We may share our testimony of faith only to be ignored or ridiculed.

God never holds us accountable for another person's decisions. Saving souls and changing lives is the work of the Spirit, well beyond our human capabilities. Although we partner with God in living out the kingdom in our relationships, we are but workers in his field. We do our best to sow good seed and tend to each other's needs, but the harvest belongs to God.

Week Three

Heavenly Father, I confess I often shirk my responsibilities to be your instrument of love and help in the world around me. Like Cain, I deny my responsibility so later I can escape guilt over a bad outcome. Teach me how to sow good seed in every circumstance and to recognize the holy work you have for me in every relationship. Help me establish healthy boundaries so that I can be of use to you without taking your place as Lord of the Harvest. Amen

Dig Deeper: Psalm 121; 1 Corinthians 3:6-9

Reflect: In which areas of my life do I take on too much "keeper" responsibility? Where do I take on too little?

Thought for Today: We are accountable for tending our relationships but not for the decisions others make.

Thursday

Firm Footing

Come quickly, LORD, and answer me, for my depression deepens. Don't turn away from me, or I will die. Let me hear of your unfailing love each morning, for I am trusting you. Show me where to walk, for I give myself to you. Rescue me from my enemies, LORD; I run to you to hide me. Teach me to do your will, for you are my God. May your gracious Spirit lead me forward on a firm footing. (Psalm 143:7-10 NLT)

Like so many psalms of David, this one is a cry to God for rescue. The psalmist feels overwhelmed by enemies to the point of desperation and despair. Knowing he can do nothing to save himself, he has two choices. He can surrender his life in defeat to his enemies, or he can take hold of the God he has learned to trust.

We know from experience how life's troubles can build to the point of crushing us. Financial difficulties, disease or disability, strained relationships, impossible expectations—these stressors weigh us down and sap our strength. The psalmist's prayer reveals four strategic steps we can take when we find ourselves similarly desperate.

1. "Show me where to walk, for I give myself to you." Our first step is to admit our need for God. We may have been following our own agenda in pride and self-sufficiency, but our troubles have humbled us. **We surrender our will to God and ask him to redirect our steps.**

2. "Rescue me from my enemies, LORD; I run to you to hide me." The enemies we face may be external forces, such as religious or political persecution, loss of economic security, or personal attacks from people we know. We may also feel attacked from within by emotional and psychological enemies, such as depression, anxiety, addiction, greed, jealousy, or persistent memories of trauma or abuse. **We ask God to protect us and fight for us against all our enemies, whether external or internal.**

3. "Teach me to do your will, for you are my God." When enemies overwhelm us, they seem to have control over our lives. They crush our will and leave us feeling hopeless until we remember that our God is sovereign over all, including our enemies and our desperate circumstances. **We reaffirm God's divine authority over our lives and ask him to show us how to live as children of light.**

4. "Lead me forward on firm footing." Desperate situations can be paralyzing. We don't know where to turn, what to do next, so we remain where we are, trapped and fearful. Like David, however, we can remember how our faithful God has rescued us before. **We call upon our trust in God to help us step forward with confidence and integrity.**

Heavenly Father, when I am beset by enemies, either from without or from within, give me the grace I need to humble myself and seek your help. Redirect my confused and desperate heart to follow your ways and trust your promises. Give me eyes to see the path you have laid out for me and faith to take my first steps, confident that you will lead me forward on a firm footing. Amen

   Dig Deeper: Matthew 7:24-25; 1 Corinthians 10:13

   Reflect: When troubles threaten me, what keeps me from asking God for rescue?

   Thought for Today: When life seems shaky, God leads us forward on a firm footing.

Friday

Why Not Gossip?

> Therefore you have no excuse, O man, every one of you who judges. For in passing judgment on another you condemn yourself, because you, the judge, practice the very same things. (Romans 2:1 ESV)

Gossip is not a modern phenomenon. Researchers have even suggested there is an evolutionary advantage in sharing information about those in our social circles. People who are most observant, so the reasoning goes, amass details about who in the tribe is trustworthy, desirable, has valuable resources, or poses a threat. Collecting and sharing information about members of a community can therefore avert danger, keep people from misbehaving, and enhance social bonding.

   Regardless of whether this thesis is valid, no one would deny that gossip can also be quite harmful. Over 57 times the Bible directly warns against the dangers of gossiping. In fact, Proverbs 6 names gossip among the seven things that God hates, along with murder, arrogance, and plotting wickedness against a brother or sister.

   If we don't want to be guilty of gossip that harms, we need to understand what gossip is and how we can avoid it.

Webster's dictionary defines gossip as the habitual practice of revealing personal and sensational facts about others. These "facts" can take one of three forms:

Lies. Arguably the worst form of gossip is telling outright lies about another person.

Half-truths. Even if the information we share is partially true, we deceive by leaving out vital facts. Telling a half-truth is the same as telling a half-lie and manipulates others by misleading them.

Truths. This is the tricky one. We can tell the absolute, whole truth about someone and it still qualifies as gossip. Why? Because our motives are selfish. We often share information as a way of solidifying our status with others as the person "in the know." Francis Bacon once observed that knowledge is power. Insider information is powerful, indeed.

Sometimes we have legitimate reasons for sharing information we've learned about someone else. We can test our motives by asking discerning questions:

- Who will benefit if I share this information?
- Am I certain of my facts?
- Do I have this person's permission to share information?
- Will anyone be worse off if I keep silent or if I speak?
- Is the timing right for sharing this information?
- Would I want such information shared about me?
- Am I seeking attention for myself by disclosing this information?
- Will sharing this information stir up discord in any way?

Until we are certain that our motives are unselfish and the benefits of sharing information are in keeping with God's desires for the community, it's probably best to keep insider information to ourselves.

Heavenly Father, help me to be a good steward of information I receive about others. Guide me in all truth and wisdom so that I may know when to speak, how to speak, and when to keep silent. Expose my pride and my efforts to gain stature with others by sharing information that does not need to be shared. Where I have sinned by gossiping, give me grace and courage to ask forgiveness from those I have injured. Amen

Dig Deeper: Proverbs 26:20; 1 Timothy 5:13

Reflect: In what context or with what person am I most likely to gossip? Why?

Thought for Today: Speak truth about others in love and service and not for selfish gain.

Saturday/Sunday

Weekend Review

Settle in: I quiet myself and acknowledge God's presence. I offer God my time and attention. I ask the Spirit to help me review my week with clarity and understanding.

Review with gratitude: I allow memories of the week to flow through me like a slow river. I notice special moments and gifts, large and small, for which I am thankful. I take some time to acknowledge these blessings before God and express my gratitude.

Celebrate: I recall what went well for me this week.

- When did I experience life-giving feelings, such as joy, peace, love, generosity, or being on a right path?
- When did I feel God's nearness?
- How did I practice new insights from my forgiveness work this week?

- In what ways did God counsel and help me this week?

Confront: I recall what did not go well for me thisweek.

- When did I experience life-draining feelings, such as anger, anxiety, envy, sadness, fear, rebelliousness, or being on a wrong path?
- When did God seem most distant?
- What forgiveness practices did I find difficult or impossible?
- In what ways did I resist God's counsel and help this week?

Talk it over: I talk with God about what I've discovered.

- I praise and thank God for the work of his Spirit in my life this week.
- I acknowledge areas of my life where I am resistant to God's call and counsel.
- I ask God for the grace I need to continue this journey of forgiving and practicing God's ways in my relationships.

Close with prayer: I pray along with this prayer of William Temple (1881-1944):

O Blessed Jesus, you know the impurity of our affection, the narrowness of our sympathy, and the coldness of our love; take possession of our souls and fill our minds with the image of yourself; break the stubbornness of our selfish wills and mold us in the likeness of your unchanging love, O you who alone can do this, our Savior, our Lord and our God. Amen

Week Four

Monday

Kingdom Righteousness

His disciples gathered around him, and he began to teach them...."But I warn you—unless your righteousness is better than the righteousness of the teachers of religious law and the Pharisees, you will never enter the Kingdom of Heaven!" (Matthew 5:20 NLT)

Followers of God long for righteousness. We try to live moral and upright lives. We give our tithes, volunteer our time, and perform useful services in the pursuit of God's favor. Despite what we know about sin, we cling to a secret hope that if we try hard enough, we can achieve a level of goodness that will meet God's standards and justify our lives.

With similar reasoning, the scribes and Pharisees of Jesus' time sought righteousness for themselves by strictly observing some 613 rules derived from Old Testament law. Then Jesus came along and pointed out critical differences between the self-righteousness practiced by these religious leaders and the kingdom righteousness that God requires.

- The self-righteous depend on the SELF to meet God's standard of goodness through personal effort. The kingdom-righteous depend on JESUS to cover their sins with his righteousness, achieved through his sinless death on the cross.

- The good deeds of the self-righteous are motivated by SELF-INTEREST and the desire to earn a place in heaven. The kingdom-righteous are motivated by LOVE and the desire to be like Jesus.

- The self-righteous perceive righteousness in DEGREES, adding or losing merit with God depending on their performance. The kingdom-righteous are justified with God through Christ's ONCE-AND-FOR-ALL sacrifice on the cross, complete and perfect.

Week Four

- The remedy for sin among the self-righteous is to FIX THE OUTSIDE, as though acting rightly can purify the inner self. The kingdom-righteous FIX THE INSIDE because a purified heart will generate outward behaviors that please God and align with God's purposes.

Kingdom work requires kingdom righteousness that lifts us beyond our selfish agendas and makes us effective for God's reconciling purposes in the world. Forgiveness, unity in the body of believers, kindness to our adversaries, peacemaking in the midst of conflict, healing of racial tensions and social injustices, protection for the elderly and the unborn, caring for the poor, sharing the hope of Jesus—all these kingdom concerns become our concerns when we surrender our hearts to the lordship of Christ and the wisdom of the Holy Spirit.

Heavenly Father, I struggle against the idea that my personal efforts at righteousness count for nothing in your kingdom. Show me where my pride interferes with my effectiveness for you. Cleanse me from selfish motivations and achievements that make me look good only on the outside. Thank you for the gift of your Son's righteousness that covers my unworthiness and makes me fit for your kingdom. Amen

Dig Deeper: Isaiah 64:6; John 15:4

Reflect: Which characteristics of the self-righteous Pharisee can I see in myself?

Thought for Today: We need God's righteousness to do God's work in the world.

Tuesday

An Enduring Name

And do not let the eunuch say, "I am just a dry tree." For thus says the LORD: To the eunuchs who keep my sabbaths, who choose the things that please me and hold fast my covenant, I will give, in my house and within my walls, a monument and a name better than sons and daughters; I will give them an everlasting name that shall not be cut off. (Isaiah 56:3b-5 NRSV)

Sometimes we may feel so damaged and unworthy that we believe God could not possibly want us to be part of his kingdom family.

Isaiah's passage, however, illustrates God's heart by pointing out his mercy to the lowest outcast of Jewish society. The eunuch was castrated in his youth so that he could become the trustworthy keeper of harems and protector of women in wealthy households. According to Jewish law he could never serve in the temple or even be part of the worshipping congregation. Moreover, he could never father sons, so his name and legacy would be lost without means of inheritance. He was highly valued for his specialized mode of service, but personally he was outcast and without a sense of family or future.

Many of us suffer like the eunuch from childhood wounds that make us feel damaged. Abuse and neglect may have twisted the delicate formation of our self-concept and made us feel like outcasts among "normal" others.

Alternatively, we may feel unworthy to be claimed by God because of shameful things we have done to ourselves or to others. By our own efforts, we have "mutilated" our souls into a condition that seems beyond repair or redemption and certainly unlovely to the eyes of a holy God.

Isaiah gently points out that past deeds cannot keep us from God's loving adoption. What was done to us—or what we have done to ourselves—does not weigh in the balance if we seek God with honest and obedient hearts now. By our human standards, we think we must be punished and penalized before our disgrace can be erased and God will notice us. But God measures us by different means. With him, our repentance and earnest desire to follow him today matter more than past deeds, no matter how terrible. His love purifies us to the deepest, darkest depths and makes us worthy to be called his children. His goodness is so extravagant and generous that he goes to great lengths to assure us a place of honor in his family and gives us a name that will endure for all eternity, outlasting and outshining all the dirty and shameful names by which we have called ourselves in the past.

Heavenly Father, so many times I have wanted to turn back the clock and undo the dark deeds that have put me under a cloud of shame and disgrace. Heal me from harm that was perpetrated on my innocence and cleanse me from the harm I have done to myself. Thank you for rescuing me from the destructive fallout of sin, for giving me a special place in your family and a beautiful name that will never be taken from me. Amen

Dig Deeper: John 10:28; Revelations 2:17

Reflect: Why is it important to receive a new name from God that will last for all eternity?

Thought for Today: God knows you not by the label of your sin but by his everlasting name for you.

Wednesday

Good Accounting

Let all that I am praise the LORD; may I never forget the good things he does for me. (Psalm 103:2 NLT)

We are prone to overlook many little blessings in life because we are looking for bigger and more dramatic ones.

Perhaps we have asked God to meet some critical need—deliverance from an illness or addiction, or the mending of a family rift. We may have been dealt an unfair blow and are waiting for God to make it right or at least give us a reason why it happened. At such times, we may become so focused on waiting for the big answers that we miss the smaller answers to our prayers and the simple, everyday ministrations of a Father who faithfully loves and cares for us.

We often make this same mistake in our relationships with each other. We allow our hurt and disappointment to blot out all that is good and right about people who injure or otherwise fail us. The offensive behavior becomes their main characteristic, and we become unable or unwilling to acknowledge their finer qualities. Anger and grief can narrow our perceptions and distort our memories, which is a good reason why the apostle Paul warns us not to let the sun go down while we are still angry (Ephesians 4:26).

The psalmist's remedy for this tendency toward distorted perceptions was to name the blessings he regularly received from God: mercy, healing, redemption, compassion. At times when he felt disappointed and angry at God, his list of blessings could provide a tangible reminder that God is indeed faithful and loving, and that a relationship shared with God is bigger than one's hurt—it is, in fact, infinitely precious and well worth mending.

Likewise, when we feel bitter over a relationship injury, we might help ourselves by sitting down and naming some qualities that we have admired and respected in the other person. Even acknowledging one or two qualities for which we are thankful can break through our barrier of hostility and shift our hearts from a position of accusation and rejection to one of appreciation, acceptance, and a hope of healing.

Heavenly Father, I admit that when I am angry, I am not interested in naming what is right and good about the person who offended me. At such times, I ask for your mind and heart to see this person as whole and complete, the way you do, and not merely as the source of my disappointment and pain. Help me to overlook faults in others as you overlook them in me, for the sake of your Son Jesus. Amen

Dig Deeper: Psalm 103:9-10; Proverbs 11:27; 19:11

Reflect: Do I know someone who seems to have no fine qualities? How might God see this person?

Thought for Today: A forgiving heart looks past the injury and holds the offender in a compassionate gaze.

Thursday

Forever Love

O give thanks to the LORD, for he is good; his steadfast love endures forever! (Psalm 118:1 NRSV)

How fortunate we are to be children of a Father whose loving faithfulness never expires, no matter what we do. Although we cannot *earn* God's love, by the same token we cannot *disqualify* ourselves from God's loving favor. We may ignore him, turn our backs on him and go our own way, yet our Father stays right beside us, showering us with mercy and steadfast love in blessings we are often slow to acknowledge or even recognize.

Our God's faithful attention is saturated with his goodness and light. There is no darkness in him, nothing evil or mean or selfish. We can trust in the truth he speaks to us; we can rely on his wise counsel to lead us in the right path. Unlike our human relationships, which often hurt and disappoint us, our Father's loving concern always works for our benefit, and it never quits. God is ever ready to listen to us, to help and heal and comfort us. Even though our devotion to him may wax and wane along with our emotions and circumstances, his caring for us remains forever constant and strong.

Heavenly Father, even the people who care most for me cannot match the forever love that you promise. None of us is entirely good, free from sin and selfish intentions, as you are. I know I have failed to love, failed to act with kindness, in the same ways that others have failed me. But you never fail me. Thank you for pursuing me even when I am rebellious and ungrateful. Forgive me for all the ways I have offended and grieved your fatherly heart. Anchor me in your love and make me strong in you so that I can be generous and forgiving of others. Amen

Dig Deeper: Romans 8:38-39; 1 John 1:5

Reflect: How can the assurance of God's love for me make me generous toward others?

Thought for Today: Nothing we do disqualifies us from God's loving favor.

Friday

Circumcise Your Heart

Circumcise, then, the foreskin of your heart, and do not be stubborn any longer. (Deuteronomy 10:16 NRSV)

This verse is situated in an important Old Testament passage in which God describes the essence of his relationship with his people. "You belong to Me," God says in effect. "I chose you. Physical circumcision distinguishes you from the world, but you must circumcise your hearts as well. You must 'cut off' useless and counterproductive practices of the world and instead act in ways that identify you as mine."

Like the ancient Israelites, we modern-day followers of Yahweh must also commit to acting in ways that identify us with our heavenly Father. This means examining our hearts for what remains uncircumcised—those parts that are unlike God or opposed to God's ways—and asking God to help us remove them. It is these unholy parts that cause conflict in our relationships and prevent us from being a blessing to the people God has placed in our lives.

Further down the passage, God describes two important attributes of Himself that should also characterize his spiritually circumcised people:

Yahweh is a just God, impartial and impossible to bribe (v. 17). In what ways are you unjust? Are you partial to a particular type of person and set against others (politically, racially, educationally, religiously)? How does the world, through advertising or peer pressure, bribe you to sacrifice God's ways for unholy ways that cause trouble and bear no fruit for God's kingdom?

Yahweh is a loving God, who cares for those in special need of mercy (v. 18). In what ways have you withheld love and mercy, kindness and forgiveness, from those who do not deserve grace yet desperately need it? How has God chosen you to give these good gifts to particular people in your life?

Heavenly Father, I confess to withholding parts of my life from you so that I can be lord over myself. Expose my unholy ways and give me the strength I need to cut them out of my heart. Help me shift my identity from earthly attachments to the assurance of being loved by you and chosen to bless the people you have put in my life. Amen

Dig Deeper: Romans 2:28-29; Colossians 2:11-12

Reflect: What unholy habit or attitude can I begin to cut from my life?

Thought for Today: Following God means giving up habits that make us unjust and unloving.

Saturday/Sunday

Weekend Review

Settle in: I quiet myself and acknowledge God's presence. I offer God my time and attention. I ask the Spirit to help me review my week with clarity and understanding.

Review with gratitude: I allow memories of the week to flow through me like a slow river. I notice special moments and gifts, large and small, for which I am thankful. I take some time to acknowledge these blessings before God and express my gratitude.

Celebrate: I recall what went well for me this week.

- When did I experience life-giving feelings, such as joy, peace, love, generosity, or being on a right path?

- When did I feel God's nearness?
- How did I practice new insights from my forgiveness work this week?
- In what ways did God counsel and help me this week?

Confront: I recall what did not go well for me this week.

- When did I experience life-draining feelings, such as anger, anxiety, envy, sadness, fear, rebelliousness, or being on a wrong path?
- When did God seem most distant?
- What forgiveness practices did I find difficult or impossible?
- In what ways did I resist God's counsel and help this week?

Talk it over: I talk with God about what I've discovered.

- I praise and thank God for the work of his Spirit in my life this week.
- I acknowledge areas of my life where I am resistant to God's call and counsel.
- I ask God for the grace I need to continue this journey of forgiving and practicing God's ways in my relationships.

Close with prayer: I pray along with this prayer of Susanna Wesley (1669-1742), mother of John and Charles Wesley:

Help me, O Lord, to make a true use of all disappointments and calamities in this life, in such a way that they may unite my heart more closely with you. Cause them to separate my affections from worldly things and inspire my soul with more vigor in the pursuit of true happiness. Amen

Week Five

Monday

Because We Are Dust

> He does not treat us as our sins deserve or repay us according to our iniquities. For as high as the heavens are above the earth, so great is his love for those who fear him; as far as the east is from the west, so far has he removed our transgressions from us. As a father has compassion on his children, so the LORD has compassion on those who fear him; for he knows how we are formed, he remembers that we are dust. (Psalm 103:10-14 NIV)

This psalm of David is one of the most quoted in the psalter. In beautiful language, the psalmist contrasts the greatness, goodness, and eternal nature of God with the frail and fleeting state of humanity.

In these few verses, we are told that God forgives us so completely because his love for us is so deep and steadfast. We also get a picture of God as the Father who loves us tenderly and compassionately, covering our sins with loving kindness because he knows we are weak and desperately need his mercy.

The apostle Paul urges us to extend this same loving kindness to those people who hurt and offend us and need our forgiveness: "Therefore, as God's chosen people, holy and dearly loved, clothe yourselves with compassion, kindness, humility, gentleness and patience. Bear with each other and forgive one another if any of you has a grievance against someone. Forgive as the Lord forgave you" (Colossians 3:12-13 NIV).

"Forgive as the Lord forgave you." In other words, remember that the person who injured you is mere dust, a frail human who is subject to fears and confusion, and motivated by pain and selfishness—in fact, a lot like yourself.

Week Five

A first step toward forgiving that person is to recognize your alikeness as flawed humans in desperate need of kindness and mercy. Have you ever acted selfishly, out of pain or confusion or fear, and later realized that you hurt someone and needed to be forgiven? Acknowledging and confessing that flaw in yourself can help you find the compassion you need to forgive others who have likewise harmed you.

Heavenly Father, I don't like to confess that I am mere dust, subject to selfish and weak motives that cause trouble in my relationships. Help me to acknowledge my own frailty so that I can be generous and compassionate with others who hurt and disappoint me. Thank you for your steadfast love and compassion that cover even the ugliest of my transgressions. Amen

Dig Deeper: Mark 11:25; Luke 23:34

Reflect: How can admitting my flaws make me better at forgiving?

Thought for Today: Admitting the flaws and frailties we all share as humans helps us forgive.

Tuesday

Rest Like a Child

> LORD, my heart is not proud; my eyes are not haughty. I don't concern myself with matters too great or too awesome for me to grasp. Instead, I have calmed and quieted myself, like a weaned child who no longer cries for its mother's milk. Yes, like a weaned child is my soul within me. O Israel, put your hope in the LORD—now and always. (Psalm 131 NLT)

This psalm is a song for pilgrims on their way to worship the Lord in Jerusalem. There is speculation that the author was a woman, particularly a mother who has nursed a child at her breast and so has deep experience of the weaned child's contentment and trust.

She invites us into this picture of contentment by pointing out what keeps us from resting and trusting in the Lord.

"My heart is not proud." The *heart* represents the whole person: thoughts, feelings, attitudes, and intentions. At the core of one's proud heart is the fear of being insignificant. The bigger we inflate ourselves, the more we fear exposure and the harder we must work to shore up our false sense of importance. **A humble heart** has at its core the secure knowledge that as children created and nurtured by our loving God, we are significant in every way that matters.

"My eyes are not haughty." Here the author addresses the way we treat others. "Haughty eyes" look down on others from a superior position. As with a proud heart, there is a core of uneasiness in this arrogant viewpoint. We cannot rest if we are constantly assessing others, looking for flaws that will make us look better by comparison. **Humble eyes** can appreciate others without measuring or judging because we know God determines our worth.

"I don't concern myself with matters too great or too awesome for me to grasp." Scripture makes it clear that God's thoughts are far above our own. Yet in prideful ambition to be like God, we challenge God's sovereignty. We judge God's performance and think we could do better. In **humble ambition**, we admit we are finite, ignorant, and utterly dependent on God's grace. Instead of overreaching our abilities, we trust God's plan for the world and look for our place in his reconciling work.

The psalmist calls on us to rest in God like a little child, no longer desperate and fearful but content in the reality of our humble dependence on an almighty God who loves and cares for us.

Heavenly Father, I am astonished to realize how many conflicts in my life can be traced to my inflated ego, arrogant disdain of others, or rebellious desire to break away from you and go my own way. Help me to learn the wisdom of humility and to give up my proud strivings that only agitate and defeat me. Teach me to find rest in your arms like a

contented child. Amen

Dig Deeper: Isaiah 55:8; Matthew 18:4

Reflect: Is there someone in my life to whom I feel superior? How do I justify my opinion?

Thought for Today: Humble eyes see value and beauty in others that haughty eyes miss.

Wednesday

Fill Up with God

> When people do not accept divine guidance, they run wild. But whoever obeys the law is joyful. (Proverbs 29:18 NLT)

Aristotle probably said it first. *Horror vacui*, or "Nature abhors a vacuum," is a natural principle we all understand. Pour water from a pitcher, and the pitcher fills with air. Extinguish a candle, and darkness replaces the light. Take God out of our lives, and ungodliness rushes in.

We see it in our nation, in our schools and our places of commerce: Wherever God is banned, Satan is glorified. Where God's law is scorned, evil and lawlessness rule. Another translation of the above proverb reads, "Where there is no word from God, people are uncontrolled" (NCV). Without the Spirit to guide us, our sinful nature takes charge and leads us into misery and destruction.

The same principle applies to our relationships. When we withhold love and grace from our interactions with others, selfishness and sin rush in to fill the gap. The result: We nurse our anger and resentment instead of seeking healing solutions. We let our tongues go wild with spiteful comments that insult and injure others. We care more about our rights and our pride than about God's heart and purpose in a difficult circumstance. In every instance where we crowd out the Spirit, we leave a space that Satan is only too glad to fill.

Happily, our proverb tells us that the reverse is also true: Satan gets crowded out by the Spirit when we seek God's guidance. Even in a hurtful and unjust circumstance, we can find joy when we obey God's law. Obedience to God fills our hearts with divine love and peace and keeps the devil from getting a destructive foothold in our relationships.

Heavenly Father, I confess that in so many little ways I exclude you from my relationships. I hoard my grudges like diamonds and guard them jealously. I lock out love and forgiveness from my heart and dwell on my injuries, savoring my pain instead of delighting in your mercy and healing solutions. Forgive me, Father. Help me to recognize the instant I turn away from you, and bring me back. Give me a heart that is repelled by my sin and desperate for the cleansing only you can provide. Amen

Dig Deeper: Deuteronomy 5:32-33; Ephesians 4:26-27

Reflect: In what small ways do I deny God access to my relationships?

Thought for Today: Reading the Bible expands God's voice in our lives and shrinks the call of sin.

Thursday

Release from Regret

> Oh, what joy for those whose disobedience is forgiven, whose sin is put out of sight! Yes, what joy for those whose record the LORD has cleared of guilt, whose lives are lived in complete honesty! (Psalm 32:1-2 NLT)

Living with regret weighs down our hearts and makes us weak. Regret is a curse we pronounce over ourselves. It is self-inflicted punishment that keeps us from experiencing the joy and peace we tell ourselves we do not deserve.

Webster's dictionary describes regret as a sorrow aroused by circumstances that are beyond one's control or power to repair. *Sorrow* is a good and necessary part of repentance; it turns our hearts toward God when we realize we cannot fix our own sin. *Regret* settles in when we choose to punish ourselves rather than seek God's mercy and accept his healing grace.

Some say the solution to the burden of regret is to forgive oneself. The real problem, however, lies in our lack of trust in God's willingness to forgive us and his ability to wash us clean. Regret is sorrow for a circumstance *beyond our control or power to repair.* This is a profound spiritual statement. Crippling regret is evidence that we don't understand or accept God's sovereignty in our lives. We displace God as judge and sentence ourselves to punishment that never ends because our sin is beyond our ability to repair. This is what it means to live under a curse.

The Bible tells us that God is sovereign not only in his role as Judge but even more as the Lover of our souls and the tender Caretaker of our lives. God's greatest joy is to forgive us and reinstate our friendship with him. If you are struggling under the tyranny of regret, try shifting your attention from ruminations about your unhappy circumstance to thoughts of God. Whenever your mind starts down that familiar dark path, purposefully turn away and think about God instead. Read a psalm. Recite the Lord's Prayer. Sing a familiar hymn of thanksgiving. Consider your blessings and realize that you have a Father who loves you and wants you to enjoy the goodness of life.

No matter what you do, God's opinion of you and his purpose for your life will not change. Because God loves you, he is committed to bringing good out of your failures and blessing out of your disobedience as you learn to trust him and recognize his work in you. God will always have the last word over your deeds because he is your sovereign Lord. He stands ready with a plan to fold your mistakes and failures into the greater design of his good purpose for you.

Heavenly Father, I still have pain over some of the things I've done that I wish I hadn't, decisions I've made that I wish I could go back and change. I've punished myself with regret over these misdeeds and unhappy circumstances, yet my sorrow lingers and will not release me. Break the chains of this curse over me, Holy Spirit. Build my faith to see that you are sovereign over my life in every way, especially over the deeds I would hide from you. Teach me to trust in your love for me so that I can receive the comfort of your forgiveness. Amen

Dig Deeper: Genesis 50:20; Matthew 11:28

Reflect: Over what circumstance in my life does regret still hold me prisoner? Why can't I let it go?

Thought for Today: Regret, like worry, is self-inflicted pain that is ultimately useless.

Friday

Choosing Sides

Now when Joshua was near Jericho, he looked up and saw a man standing in front of him with a drawn sword in his hand. Joshua went up to him and asked, "Are you for us or for our enemies?" "Neither," he replied, "but as commander of the army of the LORD I have now come." Then Joshua fell facedown to the ground in reverence, and asked him, "What message does my Lord have for his servant?" The commander of the LORD's army replied, "Take off your sandals, for the place where you are standing is holy." And Joshua did so. (Joshua 5:13-15 NIV)

We often make the mistake of thinking that, because we belong to God, he is always on our side in a quarrel or a conflict. The truth is, our belonging to God means that *we* must always be on *God's* side.

It is God's sovereign purpose, not ours, that should define our battles. Our best chance of success lies not in asking God to win our battles for us but in submitting ourselves to him and aligning ourselves along the battle lines God chooses.

We may be surprised to learn that the real battle lies not with our human adversaries but within our own minds and hearts as we face thoughts and attitudes that must be defeated, such as bitterness, anger, disappointment, fear, vengeance, or the need to control.

Heavenly Father, help me to release my quarrels and relationship problems to you. Redefine them in the light of your good and redemptive will, so that I may ask, how can I best serve God's purpose in this situation? Help me to recognize when my enemy is not the other person but rather my own thoughts and attitudes that struggle against your sovereign lordship in my life. Amen

Dig Deeper: James 4:7; Psalm 91:9-12

Reflect: Is there a conflict in my life that God would like to redefine for me?

Thought for Today: Our toughest conflicts may rage within the bounds of our own minds and hearts.

Saturday/Sunday

Weekend Review

Settle in: I quiet myself and acknowledge God's presence. I offer God my time and attention. I ask the Spirit to help me review my week with clarity and understanding.

Review with gratitude: I allow memories of the week to flow through me like a slow river. I notice special moments and gifts, large and small, for which I am thankful. I take some time to acknowledge these blessings before God and express my gratitude.

Celebrate: I recall what went well for me this week.

- When did I experience life-giving feelings, such as joy, peace, love, generosity, or being on a right path?

- When did I feel God's nearness?
- How did I practice new insights from my forgiveness work this week?
- In what ways did God counsel and help me this week?

Confront: I recall what did not go well for me this week.

- When did I experience life-draining feelings, such as anger, anxiety, envy, sadness, fear, rebelliousness, or being on a wrong path?
- When did God seem most distant?
- What forgiveness practices did I find difficult or impossible?
- In what ways did I resist God's counsel and help this week?

Talk it over: I talk with God about what I've discovered.

- I praise and thank God for the work of his Spirit in my life this week.
- I acknowledge areas of my life where I am resistant to God's call and counsel.
- I ask God for the grace I need to continue this journey of forgiving and practicing God's ways in my relationships.

Close with prayer: I pray along with this prayer of Thomas Merton (1915-1968):

My Lord God, I have no idea where I am going.

I do not see the road ahead of me.

I cannot know for certain where it will end.

Nor do I really know myself,

and the fact that I think I am following your will

does not mean I am actually doing so.

But I believe that the desire to please you does in fact please you.
And I hope I have that desire in all that I am doing.
I hope that I will never do anything apart from that desire.
And I know that if I do this you will lead me by the right road,
though I may know nothing about it.

Therefore will I trust you always
though I may seem to be lost and in the shadow of death.
I will not fear, for you are ever with me,
and you will never leave me to face my perils alone. Amen

Week Six

Monday

Reckoning Our Worth

Since we are living by the Spirit, let us follow the Spirit's leading in every part of our lives. Let us not become conceited, or provoke one another, or be jealous of one another. (Galatians 5:25-26 NLT)

Conceit and envy are flip sides of the same belief: *My value as a person depends on how well my life compares with yours.* Whether we feel superior to others or inferior, those feelings indicate an area in our lives that is still submitted to the world's leading rather than to the Spirit's.

When we live in the Spirit, we seek God's approval above anyone else's. We eagerly watch for signs that the Spirit is transforming us into the likeness of Christ, a process that strips away lies and expectations that the world lays on us and makes us available for God's work. When our value depends on God's opinion of us, we can avoid conflict with others that is rooted in jealousy and defensive behaviors meant to conceal our flaws and weaknesses.

Through Scripture God assures us that he loves and cherishes us just as he made us, with nothing added or subtracted.

Heavenly Father, make your love for me so real that I can appreciate my worth without constantly comparing myself to others. Help me to recognize when my relationship difficulties are rooted in my need to feel important and valued, and give me the grace to turn to you to get those needs met. Thank you for the cross as irrefutable proof of your deep and extravagant love for me. Amen

Dig Deeper: Psalm 139:14; 2 Corinthians 3:18; 1 John 3:1

Reflect: How has the world lied to me about my worth?

Thought for Today: We find our value not in our works but in God's work in us.

Tuesday

God's Unstoppable Purpose

For this is what the Lord says…"I make known the end from the beginning, from ancient times, what is still to come. I say, 'My purpose will stand, and I will do all that I please.'" (Isaiah 45:18; 46:10 NIV)

At times the weight of our world can seem overwhelming. Greed and dishonesty dominate the political landscape. We turn on the news only to witness another atrocity committed in our own neighborhoods or in communities on the other side of the globe. Against a rising tide of evil and moral confusion, we well may ask, *what are we to do? How would God have us respond?*

Scripture tells us to remember that our God is sovereign. Nothing happens outside of God's attention. No force can stand against God's purpose. Not only does God know how history will write itself, he unfolds it in exactly the manner and timing that he has decided.

Like a powerful train, God's will for this world is already heading toward its destination. We cannot stop it or turn it aside by anything we do. Neither can anyone else, not those who work evil and make plans in the dark to take what they want and bring harm to others. No human can stop or slow the train or alter the track on which it runs.

So, again, what are we to do when it seems that evil has the advantage over us?

The answer is to stay as close to God as possible, hiding ourselves in the shelter of his wings. We do this by following Jesus' example in three practical ways:

Make sure you're on the train with God. God allows us to choose against his will, but all other paths lead to misery and destruction. Jesus is our model for making the Father's will our own and aligning ourselves with his purpose. We can know the same peace and certainty that Jesus experienced in the face of hostility when our hearts and minds are facing forward, our gaze fixed on God, on his greatness and his unshakable plan for our good and the good of his creation.

Pray for the reign of God's kingdom on earth. "Your kingdom come. Your will be done, on earth as it is in heaven" (Matthew 6:10 NRSV). Jesus not only spoke these hopeful words but worked toward their fulfillment moment by moment, in his every interaction with people. Through his deep and constant prayer life, Jesus followed the psalmist's advice to seek God's counsel before making plans and allowing God's wisdom to foster attitudes and decisions consistent with God's great purpose.

Persist in doing good. Our natural inclination is to strike back when we've been hurt. In our humanness, we don't want to do good to those who harm us, to forgive the unrepentant, or to pray for the good of those who consider us enemies. Under God's sovereign rule, however, evil can never be defeated by evil but only by goodness. God's truth exposes the devil's whispering lies and frustrates his schemes. God's love outlasts hatred and touches the need in every human heart for compassion and forgiveness. Like Jesus, we align ourselves with God when we return kindness for insult and goodness for the evil we receive.

God's train is headed for a redeemed and perfect creation bathed constantly in his glorious presence. Because of Jesus, we are invited to board the train and share in that kingdom glory even now, right here on earth, in our everyday circumstances.

Heavenly Father, sometimes the events of this world seem overwhelming. I look for you but see only the face of evil winning and your people suffering. Help me to trust in your promise of ultimate good in this world by the incremental good we do every day. Your timing is not our timing, yet I praise you for the reality of your sovereignty over our lives and your unstoppable will that moves us steadily toward the redemption of your created world. Amen

Dig Deeper: Psalm 16:7-8; 17:8-9; Romans 1:28-32

Reflect: How might my belief in God's absolute and unshakable sovereignty reshape my response to distressing news?

Thought for Today: God's purpose in the world is sovereign, eternal, and unstoppable.

Wednesday

Recasting the Sinner

So if anyone is in Christ, there is a new creation: everything old has passed away; see, everything has become new! (2 Corinthians 5:17 NRSV)

When we confess our belief in Jesus as Lord, we are reborn into a new identity. God's gift of grace and forgiveness transforms us into children of light, beloved ones who belong to God. The Father no longer sees us as hopeless sinners but as holy image-bearers of Christ's goodness and mercy. Our offenses are overlooked under the mantle of Christ's righteousness.

Among our human relationships, however, offenses too often are spotlighted and trigger distortions in our perceptions of one another. In the moment we take offense, for example, we may redefine someone's character according to his or her offensive act. That person whom we had trusted is now a liar, a betrayer, an adulterer, a thief. An enemy. Qualities we had valued, such as thoughtfulness or cheerfulness, now seem hollow and deceptive.

We may think such negative recasting of this person's identity shields us from further harm. In fact, it cocoons us in a distorted reality that keeps us isolated, bitter, and immovable.

Forgiveness is a powerful act of grace that breaks us out of our self-made cocoon. In forgiving we recast into a positive light the person who hurt us. We begin to see a sinner much like ourselves, struggling in a world of temptation, yet so loved by God that Jesus was sent to die in this person's place. In forgiving we free ourselves to love and care for this person again, to value the positive qualities we once recognized, and to envision a new relationship unstained by the offense or our unmet expectations.

Heavenly Father, you have covered my sins with the righteous blood of Jesus, yet I have been selfish with the grace and mercy you shower on me. Help me to be generous with those who sin against me, remembering that your love is infinite and your mercy is meant to be shared. I pray for the desire to overlook offenses and to be the love and light of Christ in all my relationships. Amen

Dig Deeper: Psalm 32:1-2; 103:12; 2 Corinthians 5:18-20

Reflect: How can being created new in Christ make a difference in my relationships?

Thought for Today: Forgiveness is powerful because it recasts sinners in a positive light.

Thursday

You Are My Witnesses

> "You are my witnesses," declares the LORD, "and my servant whom I have chosen, so that you may know and believe me and understand that I am he. Before me no god was formed, nor will there be one after me. I, even I, am the LORD, and apart from me there is no savior." (Isaiah 43:10-11 NIV)

In a court of law, witnesses play an important role. Witnesses provide a bridge between an unfamiliar event and the people (jurors or judges) who must render a decision about it. A witness's value lies in his or her personal experience of the event in question, even when that experience is limited or not fully understood by the witness. A testimony that is limited but nevertheless truthful helps the court toward an accurate perception of the event, leading to conclusions that are reasonable and just.

The Isaiah passage quoted above was written to Jews living in exile in Babylon. God tells them they are in a perfect position to be his witnesses. God chose the Jews to share with their new neighbors everything they knew about God—how God's prophecies had been proven true and how God cared for their ancestors in the wilderness. "Explain to them," God says, "your hope in Me as your only God and Savior."

Before his ascension, Jesus commissioned all believers to continue this mission of being God's witnesses in the world. If you are a follower of Christ, then you have been chosen by God to give true and faithful testimony of your experience to the people in your life for whom God's saving grace is an unfamiliar event. You are the bridge God is providing them to make himself known.

Three assets qualified the Jews to be witnesses in Babylon: *knowing* God (personal experience), *believing* God (trust and faith), and *understanding* God (recognizing the nature, significance, and purpose of God as Creator, Sustainer, Redeemer, and King). Jesus gives us a fourth asset in the *Holy Spirit*, who guides and empowers us to be true and faithful witnesses, even though our experience of God is limited and our understanding finite.

Heavenly Father, help me to be a true witness for you in the relationships you have given me. Build in me a knowledge, belief, and understanding of your divine Self so that my witness will be accurate. Thank you for your Spirit, who gives life and power to my witness, making it an effective bridge to those who don't know you. Amen

Dig Deeper: Acts 1:8; 1 Peter 3:15

Reflect: What personal experience of God am I willing to share with others?

Thought for Today: Our limited yet faithful witness helps people know and believe God.

Friday

Living on the Edge

> Since you have heard about Jesus and have learned the truth that comes from him, throw off your old sinful nature and your former way of life, which is corrupted by lust and deception. Instead, let the Spirit renew your thoughts and attitudes. Put on your new nature, created to be like God—truly righteous and holy. (Ephesians 4:21-24 NLT)

Day by day—even moment by moment—we face the choice of living under heaven's rule or the rule of the world.

When we choose to follow Christ, we receive a new nature and the indwelling Spirit as evidence that we belong to God. As God reshapes our hearts and resets our priorities and desires, we begin to feel at odds with our old, sinful nature. Still, our old nature persists and challenges our new desire to live according to God's ways. We feel this tension between our two natures especially at our testing points, or our *spiritual edges*—those uncomfortable places where we long to follow Christ but also feel that strong pull for the things of this world.

To live on our spiritual edge means to live consciously and honestly, aware of our testing points and the spiritual significance of our choices. The Holy Spirit meets us at these edges, teaching, challenging, and encouraging us. Some tests we face are quite simple while others are difficult and complicated, especially if they touch on our deepest fears, unfulfilled needs, or painful memories. Keep in mind, our sinful nature supports any decision that keeps us comfortable in a world that opposes God's rule. Consequently, we may resist telling the truth if it means losing face or financial security; we may cling to resentment when a friend or relative abuses our trust; or we might make excuses for behaviors that hurt our relationships, instead of asking for forgiveness.

Despite the difficulty of these tests and the pain of failing them, we can be thankful for them because our spiritual edges are precisely where God is working to grow our faith and mature us into holy perfection. Each decision, big or small, that we make *toward* God and his kingdom adds cumulatively to our Christian character and solidifies our identity as one who belongs to God. Indeed, God promises that these decisions will endure and follow us into eternity as we make our forever home with him (Revelation 14:13).

Heavenly Father, I acknowledge the spiritual edges in my life, those situations and relationships where I struggle and so often fail to live according to your ways. Help me to see these testing areas as evidence of your steadfast love for me and your desire to see me righteous and holy like Jesus. Thank you for sending your Spirit Counselor to advise and encourage me and to catch me when I stumble. Give me faith, dear Father, and the courage and wisdom to make even the smallest decisions count toward your glory and my eternal joy in your kingdom. Amen

Dig Deeper: Colossians 3:10; Psalm 37:23-24

Reflect: In what area of my life does my sin nature tend to pull me away from God?

Thought for Today: Faith helps us to desire God's ways more than the ways of the world.

Saturday/Sunday

Weekend Review

Settle in: I quiet myself and acknowledge God's presence. I offer God my time and attention. I ask the Spirit to help me review my week with clarity and understanding.

Review with gratitude: I allow memories of the week to flow through me like a slow river. I notice special moments and gifts, large and small, for which I am thankful. I take some time to acknowledge these blessings before God and express my gratitude.

Celebrate: I recall what went well for me this week.

- When did I experience life-giving feelings, such as joy, peace, love, generosity, or being on a right path?
- When did I feel God's nearness?
- How did I practice new insights from my forgiveness work this week?
- In what ways did God counsel and help me this week?

Confront: I recall what did not go well for me this week.

- When did I experience life-draining feelings, such as anger, anxiety, envy, sadness, fear, rebelliousness, or being on a wrong path?
- When did God seem most distant?
- What forgiveness practices did I find difficult or impossible?
- In what ways did I resist God's counsel and help this week?

Talk it over: I talk with God about what I've discovered.

- I praise and thank God for the work of his Spirit in my life this week.
- I acknowledge areas of my life where I am resistant to God's call and counsel.
- I ask God for the grace I need to continue this journey of forgiving and practicing God's ways in my relationships.

Close with prayer: I pray along with this prayer of John Baillie (1886-1960):

O God my Creator and Redeemer, I may not go forth today except You accompany me with Your blessing....Speak in my words today, think in my thoughts, and work in all my deeds. And seeing that it is Your gracious will to make use even of such weak human instruments in the fulfillment of Your mighty purpose for the world, let my life today be the channel through which some little portion of Your divine love and pity may reach the lives that are nearest to my own. Amen

Week Seven

Monday

The Danger in Blessings

I thought, "Surely I will die surrounded by my family after a long, good life. For I am like a tree whose roots reach the water, whose branches are refreshed with the dew. New honors are constantly bestowed on me, and my strength is continually renewed." (Job 29:18-20 NLT)

Is there such a thing as being too blessed? Can an abundance of good things be bad for us?

Like Job, we can get so comfortable in the goodness of our lives that we expect our blessings to continue indefinitely. A sudden crisis will then take us by surprise and throw our faith into a tailspin. Like Job, we might metaphorically shake our fist at God and demand an explanation. "Why this, God? How could you let this happen? I thought you loved me."

How we attend to our blessings can predict how we will respond to a crisis. Do we take the time to notice all the ways that God loves and cares for us on a daily basis? Are we grateful, or have repeated blessings merely raised our level of expectation?

We can attend to our blessings in three different ways:

- Focusing on the BLESSED (Me) leads me into a sense of entitlement. I believe I somehow deserve blessings and expect to continue receiving them. When crisis strikes, I feel betrayed, hurt, and angry. I doubt God's love for me and question God's trustworthiness.

- Focusing on the BLESSING (the Good Thing) leads me into greed and addiction. I want more and more good things because my happiness depends on them. When crisis strikes, I feel scared and deprived. I blame God for being cruel and look for ways to recover what I have lost.

- Focusing on the BLESSOR (God) leads me into humility and

gratitude. The goodness I experience reinforces my understanding of God's good and loving nature and generous care of his creation. When crisis strikes, I remember how much God loves me. I stay open to God and trust the Holy Spirit to lead me through the crisis.

This same principle applies to blessings and crises in our human relationships. When we are in the habit of accepting goodness from others without much thought, we are apt to turn resentful or anxious when the goodness stops flowing. If, however, we take time to notice the gifts and appreciate the givers, we will be better equipped to handle the inevitable human failings and frustrations when they come along.

Heavenly Father, I fail to recognize the blessings you shower on me every day. I go about my business expecting goodness to surround me as though it is my right. Forgive me for taking your good gifts and not noticing your loving hand reaching out to me. Thank you for the people in my life who give to me so generously; temper my selfishness with humility and gratitude for them. Amen

Dig Deeper: 2 Kings 6:15-17; Psalm 145:13-16

Reflect: How might memorizing Scripture help me prepare for a crisis?

Thought for Today: How we handle our blessings can predict how we handle a crisis.

Tuesday

Quality Faith

Then the disciples came to Jesus in private and asked, "Why couldn't we drive [the demon] out [of the boy]?" He replied, "Because you have so little faith. Truly I tell you, if you have faith as small as a mustard seed, you can say to this mountain, 'Move from here to there,' and it will move. Nothing will be impossible for you." (Matthew 17:19-20 NIV)

Like the disciples, we sometimes wonder why our spiritual lives are not more effective. We love and believe in God, so why do we so often fall prey to worry and fear, anger and resentment? What keeps us from living the sure and steadfast life that God desires for us?

Jesus would answer us in the same way he answered his disciples: It's not the size of your faith that matters but its nature. Even small faith of the purest quality can achieve amazing results.

Quality faith—the kind that can move mountains—is a gift from God that only comes to us through relationship with God. Difficult circumstances test our faith for its character and purity. When adversity strikes, doubts about God's goodness, power, and concern for us can derail our faith and make our prayers ineffective. These same adversities, however, can work for our good when we use them as a springboard for practicing new ways to rely on God.

In the face of adversity, we can practice a new approach:

- Redefine the adversity as an opportunity to learn more about depending on God.

- Offer a simple prayer: "Lord, I look to you instead of myself for the solution to this dilemma."

- Pause to rest in the peace of God's presence and remember that we are God's beloved.

- Try God's way instead the familiar way of the world.

- Adopt God's vision to see people instead of merely a conflict.

- Forgive an adversary when we would rather hold a grudge.

- Risk the world's disapproval because we want to please God.

Week Seven

Heavenly Father, like the disciples in Jesus' day, I have doubts that keep me from trusting you with my whole heart. Give me courage to risk new ways of responding to conflict and adversity. Purify my faith so that I might be Christ's power and presence in my relationships. Amen

Dig Deeper: Matthew 8:26; James 1:2-4

Reflect: In what area of my life does God want to build my trust in him?

Thought for Today: Trusting God in the face of adversity purifies our faith.

Wednesday

Blessed Gifting

Remember the words of the Lord Jesus, how he himself said, "It is more blessed to give than to receive." (Acts 20:35b ESV)

The idea that giving is better than receiving makes intuitive sense. Think of the joy you've experienced when giving a gift to someone you care about. Much of the fun of celebrating birthdays and holidays is in surprising and pleasing others with our offerings.

Some offerings, however, may seem too costly to bestow freely. Consider what it means, for example, to forgive someone who has wronged you or to grant a second chance to someone who has abused your trust. What do we sacrifice in refusing to gossip about someone who has behaved shamefully or in overlooking an offense that has cost us emotionally or financially? Sometimes such gifts feel beyond our capacity, or even our *desire*, to afford them.

Moreover, when we have suffered a personal wound, we may feel entitled to receive a gift *first*—an apology, restitution, or at least an admission of wrongdoing—before we will consider offering our own gift. Stubborn stalemates keep our relationships locked in hurt and anger and prevent those changes we need to heal and grow.

God's antidote for a stubborn stalemate is love. Love motivates us to offer gifts when we would rather be on the receiving end. Because of love we can honor others above ourselves, even when we think they don't deserve such treatment. Love reminds us that God forgives and accepts us without reserve, despite our every selfish act and evil intention.

We are blessed when we sacrifice pride and self-interest in order to give good gifts to others. Such obedience pleases our Father because it makes us more like Christ in character and intent.

Heavenly Father, thank you for pouring out your love on me without reserve. At those times when I am tempted to hold out for payment from someone who has wronged me, help me to visualize Jesus on the cross, loving me with the greatest gift he could offer. Give me the grace I need to extend my hand, not to receive but to give, and to look for your blessing. Amen

Dig Deeper: Romans 12:10; Philippians 2:3-4; 1 Peter 4:8

Reflect: When has someone loved me with a reconciling gift I did not deserve?

Thought for Today: Love offers forgiveness where it is undeserved.

Thursday

Love Never Fails

Love never fails. (1 Corinthians 13:8 NKJV)

The apostle Paul tells us that "love never fails" in the sense that love is eternal and imperishable. Love is always steadfast and sure; it bears all things and never gives up. Love cannot be destroyed by circumstances or disasters, injuries or betrayals. It is solid as a rock, immovable, dependable. It cannot be corrupted by sin or desire; it does not succumb to pressure or fade away. Even when all else fails, love remains.

Can we know such love as this?

The love Paul describes is perfect love, God's kind of love. In fact, the above paragraph is a good description of God Himself. This makes sense because, as the apostle John wrote, God *is* love. God showed us his love, his heart, when Jesus walked the earth and modeled for us what it means to love God and each other with deep and unfailing love.

Human love, on the other hand, does fail because it is by nature self-focused. We tend to love with an eye to our own interests. We love jealously, selfishly, manipulatively. Our love is easily provoked to anger and hurt when our desires and appetites are not met. We want proof that we are important and appreciated, so our love keeps a record of wrongs. It may resort to deception or infidelity to satisfy its cravings.

God commands us to love one another but with *his* kind of love. Our human love is insufficient for the kingdom work God assigns us. Fortunately, by his miraculous and wonderful plan, God fills us with his perfect love as we grow in faith and become more like Jesus. When God's kind of love rules our hearts, grace rules our relationships. We can look past ourselves and reach out to one who has been hurtful and say, "I care for you. I won't give up on you. I forgive you."

Heavenly Father, your love for me is so deep and amazing that it is beyond my understanding. That you could give me such love to share with others is an honor and privilege I do not take lightly. In the midst of trouble and conflict, help me to reach past my poor human love and extend your kind of love to others. Give me the will to overlook my own interests and dismiss my record of wrongs so that I can love and forgive the people you bring into my life. Amen

Dig Deeper: Song of Songs 8:7; 1 John 4:7-8

Reflect: What are three clues that tell me I am loving with human love and not with God's kind of love?

Thought for Today: When God's love rules our hearts, grace rules our relationships.

Friday

Love Turned Bitter

> As the ark of the LORD was entering the City of David, Michal daughter of Saul watched from a window. And when she saw King David leaping and dancing before the LORD, she despised him in her heart. (2 Samuel 6:16 NIV)

Bitterness often draws its energy from a love betrayed or a loyalty or trust that was abused. We may get annoyed or even angry at a stranger, but we rarely feel bitter. Bitterness takes hold of us in proportion to the depth of our passion—if we love deeply, our bitterness will be sharp and difficult to dislodge.

In the above passage, Michal's love for her husband, David, had soured into bitterness. The hero she had once admired and protected returned after many years with new wives and children, while she remained alone and childless. At the sight of him her heart hardened, and she despised him.

Bitterness serves us by putting up a wall around our unwanted feelings—sorrow, disappointment, humiliation, sometimes even our own guilt. It shields us from pain by focusing our attention on the one who hurt us. Bitterness, however, can never heal a broken heart. In fact, bitterness works against our healing by keeping the wound fresh and our thoughts trapped in a vicious spiral of hopeless anger and hurt.

Our best chance for healing lies in shifting our attention away from our wounded heart to dwell on the grace and tenderness of God. Bitterness loses some of its sting when we remember how deeply and steadfastly our heavenly Father loves and cares for us. We won't need our bitterness to shield us when we receive our sense of value from God instead of from the person who let us down.

Heavenly Father, you know how trapped I sometimes feel by the injustice and hurt of someone's ill treatment of me. I can't seem to get past my resentment over the unfairness of it all. But I know that wallowing in my anger and pain is not the life you want for me. Give me the desire and courage to put aside my bitter feelings. Teach me how to live upright and joyful despite how others may treat me. Help me to find peace in you despite unpleasant circumstances. Amen

Dig Deeper: Ezekiel 11:19-20; Psalm 25:4-5

Reflect: How does bitterness protect me?

Thought for Today: Bitterness encases us in our pain so we cannot heal.

Saturday/Sunday

Weekend Review

Settle in: I quiet myself and acknowledge God's presence. I offer God my time and attention. I ask the Spirit to help me review my week with clarity and understanding.

Review with gratitude: I allow memories of the week to flow through me like a slow river. I notice special moments and gifts, large and small, for which I am thankful. I take some time to acknowledge these blessings before God and express my gratitude.

Celebrate: I recall what went well for me this week.

- When did I experience life-giving feelings, such as joy, peace, love, generosity, or being on a right path?
- When did I feel God's nearness?
- How did I practice new insights from my forgiveness work this week?
- In what ways did God counsel and help me this week?

Confront: I recall what did not go well for me this week.

- When did I experience life-draining feelings, such as anger, anxiety, envy, sadness, fear, rebelliousness, or being on a wrong path?
- When did God seem most distant?
- What forgiveness practices did I find difficult or impossible?
- In what ways did I resist God's counsel and help this week?

Talk it over: I talk with God about what I've discovered.

- I praise and thank God for the work of his Spirit in my life this week.
- I acknowledge areas of my life where I am resistant to God's call and counsel.
- I ask God for the grace I need to continue this journey of forgiving and practicing God's ways in my relationships.

Close with prayer: Pray along with this prayer of Martin Luther (1483-1546):

Dear God, I have been wronged. Why?

I do not deserve it of this person.

But I must remember and understand who I am to you.

There is a long complaint against me,

proving that I am ten times worse

and have sinned a thousand times more against you

than my neighbor has against me.

Therefore I must agree with your wish by sincerely praying:

O Lord, forgive, and I will also forgive. Amen.

Week Eight

Monday

Looking for Grace

My purpose in writing is to encourage you and assure you that what you are experiencing is truly part of God's grace for you. Stand firm in this grace. (1 Peter 5:12b NLT)

God's wisdom teaches us to look for his grace in every circumstance, even the most difficult and painful ones.

It's easy to recognize God's loving care in the blessings we receive, in circumstances that make us feel happy and secure and fortunate. But what about when disaster hits or when systems beyond our control threaten us? Where is God when relationships fail despite our best efforts or when our obedience to him brings on ridicule and persecution?

We don't easily recognize God's grace in a difficult circumstance. We may even conclude that God doesn't really care and has abandoned us altogether.

At such times, we must remember to think with the mind of Christ and not rely on the world's wisdom. Through faith we know that God is sovereign, which means that he has either ordained or permitted every circumstance in our lives. It also means that there are many circumstances he has *not* permitted. We will never know all the dangers from which God has secretly rescued us, all the times we were kept safe because God sent his angels to defend and protect us.

Biblical wisdom tells us that God has already thought through all possibilities and, in his gracious love, has chosen to allow only those circumstances that can work for our ultimate good if we choose, as Jesus did, to remain steadfast in our faith. God knows exactly how each test or temptation can teach us something new about obedience and relying on him for our strength and direction. As Christ on earth learned obedience from what he suffered, we too are perfected and made holy as we view our trials through the lens of God's grace and mercy and learn to stand firm in them.

Heavenly Father, I confess I don't like the idea of suffering and would rather avoid it if possible. When trials do come, however, teach me how to stay close to you and draw strength from your love. Give me wisdom to eventually see how this particular test or suffering can teach me something I need to know and could learn in no other way. Help me to see through the lie that my suffering is proof that you don't care; teach me instead to recognize your grace in every circumstance you allow in my life. Amen

Dig Deeper: 1 Corinthians 2:16; Hebrews 5:8; 1 Peter 5:6-7

Reflect: How might looking for God's grace change my attitude toward a current situation in my life?

Thought for Today: Even a painful situation bears the imprint of God's grace and love for you.

Tuesday

God Builds Us Up

> Then the Lord gave me this message…"I will watch over and care for them, and I will bring them back here again. I will build them up and not tear them down. I will plant them and not uproot them." (Jeremiah 24:4, 6 NLT)

It's unhealthy and hurtful but we've all experienced it—the temptation to build ourselves up by tearing others down, to prove our superiority by exposing another person's flaws. Sometimes the barbs are subtle—an innocuous comment that nevertheless stings because it hints at an insult. Other attacks are more blatant—a well-aimed criticism that targets a known weakness or injury, leaving the victim angry and embarrassed.

If we grew up in families where these tactics were used to manipulate power, then we probably expect God to act in much the same way. Consequently, we hide our weaknesses from God for fear he will use them against us. We pretend to be perfect so God will not shame or reject us.

What we don't realize is that God doesn't need to prove his superiority at our expense. His love for us is pure, uncomplicated by sinful pride or latent feelings of inferiority. Our Father God desires only that we present ourselves—our *whole* selves—for his care and nurture so that he can protect and comfort us, heal and enjoy us.

Heavenly Father, every relationship in my life has had its share of stings and barbs and efforts to manipulate. I confess that sometimes I was the victim, and sometimes I was the aggressor. Search my heart and show me the tender areas that trigger my need to bolster my ego at the expense of others. Give me faith to trust in your love so that I can be whole and real in your presence. Shield me from the hurtful manipulations of others, and help me to forgive them as you expose the same weaknesses in me. Amen

Dig Deeper: Nahum 1:7; Romans 14:19; 1 Peter 5:6-7

Reflect: How did my family experiences shape my view of God?

Thought for Today: God will never abuse our efforts to be wholly honest before him.

Wednesday

Seeds for Sowing

Everyone should give whatever they have decided in their heart. They shouldn't give with hesitation or because of pressure. God loves a cheerful giver. God has the power to provide you with more than enough of every kind of grace. That way, you will have everything you need always and in everything to provide more than enough for every kind of good work. (2 Corinthians 9:7-8 CEB)

To the modern church-goer, this passage will be familiar as the text pastors like to quote during fundraising campaigns. Indeed, Paul is appealing to the Corinthian church to dig into their pockets and donate money to help the poor and persecuted believers in Jerusalem. He uses the common illustration of agriculture to make his point: The farmer who scatters only a little seed reaps a meager crop, but a generous sower will reap a bountiful harvest.

Generosity is a biblical theme that extends well beyond financial giving. Every grace that we receive gives us a store of "seed" we can turn around and invest in other people. God promises enough grace to satisfy our needs and "more than enough" to share with others in doing Christ's good work of loving and helping one another.

The principle is simple but profound: As you are given grace, give grace generously to others. Little graces come our way every day—kindness from a stranger, patience from someone inconvenienced by our mistake, forgiveness from a friend we have offended, compassion when we are hurting. These little seeds find their way into our hearts if we are humble and open to receiving them. There they set down roots and produce more seed after their own kind, available for us to share. This miraculous process is powered and directed by God's Spirit, from whom all grace abounds: "The one who supplies seed for planting and bread for eating will supply and multiply your seed and will increase your crop, which is righteousness" (2 Corinthians 9:10 CEB).

Seed that sits in our pockets is wasted. If we are stingy with our kindness, if we withhold patience and forgiveness from those who do not "deserve" them, then we likely will raise up cold and fruitless relationships. If, however, we offer compassion instead of judgment and mercy instead of punishment, if we invest ourselves in trying to understand rather than demanding to be understood, then God will raise up blessings in our midst. The seeds that changed us will take root in hearts near to us, perhaps to flourish and bless us in return.

When you feel relief because your debt has been forgiven, let that gratitude spur you to forgive another who is burdened with guilt. Notice the kindnesses that help you make it through the day. Study them, practice them, and multiply them in your relationships. See what harvest the Lord will give you when you sow grace generously into the good soil of the people around you.

Heavenly Father, I confess I have been too cautious in sharing kindness and forgiveness with others, as if grace were so scarce I dare not squander it. Thank you for your continuous flow of blessings to me, though I am undeserving and often ungrateful. Holy Spirit, soften my heart until I am open and humble enough to receive your seeds of grace. Multiply these graces in me and teach me to share them freely and indiscriminately. Amen

Dig Deeper: Proverbs 11:25; Ephesians 4:32

Reflect: Of the graces I have recently received, which meant the most to me? With whom could I share these graces?

Thought for Today: Sow seeds of grace generously to reap a bountiful harvest in your relationships.

Thursday

Sinner or Saint?

O God, you take no pleasure in wickedness; you cannot tolerate the sins of the wicked. Therefore, the proud may not stand in your presence, for you hate all who do evil. (Psalm 5:4-5 NLT)

In this prayer for the morning, David reflects on a classic theme found among the wisdom writings of the Old Testament. He describes a strong demarcation between the godly and the wicked of the world, between the righteous whom God loves and their lying enemies whom God abhors.

If we are honest, we must admit that this line of demarcation is not as clear as David describes it. We ourselves regularly appear on both sides of the righteousness issue: faithful and then unfaithful, truthful and then hiding behind a protective veil of deceit.

Who among the righteous, for example, could never identify with the wicked as David goes on to describe: "My enemies cannot speak a truthful word. Their deepest desire is to destroy others. Their talk is foul, like the stench from an open grave. Their tongues are filled with flattery" (Psalm 5:9 NLT).

His description sounds dramatic, yet we know from experience that gossip and slander are indeed foul and damaging to relationships. Hollow praise sows mistrust and can derail good works. Jesus tells his disciples that the desire to sin against others is just as harmful as acting on that desire because sinful intentions corrode our minds and hearts.

Consequently, who among us does not deserve the punishment David asks for in verse 10: "O God, declare them guilty. Let them be caught in their own traps. Drive them away because of their many sins, for they have rebelled against you." David calls on God to punish the wicked by their own deeds and banish them from God's holy presence. For the righteous, however, he asks a blessing: "But let all who take refuge in you rejoice; let them sing joyful praises forever. Spread your protection over them, that all who love your name may be filled with joy" (v. 11).

Fortunately, God does not accept or reject us based on our ability to achieve perfection but on whether we love his name and take refuge in the saving grace of Jesus Christ. The line of demarcation David describes runs right through each of us. The line casts us as creatures of both light and darkness, who can desire to do good as well as to sin, and who follow God for a time but then stray into selfish and hurtful ways.

The Good News of Jesus is that his atoning sacrifice covers our whole being, leaving no part of us unredeemed and unfit for God's holy presence. Not only are we saved for eternal life but we also receive the Holy Spirit, who works tirelessly to refine us and shrink the power of darkness and sin over our deeds and desires.

Heavenly Father, I indulge in the comforting notion that there is a strong difference between me and the wicked people of the world. Teach me the folly of elevating myself to a status of righteousness I do not deserve without the grace of Jesus. Show me the line of demarcation running through my own life and help me to live more and more in your light and truth. Amen

Dig Deeper: Matthew 5:27-30; 1 John 1:5-7

Reflect: In what area(s) of my life am I most likely to cross the line from light into darkness?

Thought for Today: God abhors our wickedness, but Jesus covers us with his righteousness.

Friday

Fruitful Prayer

> Then Jesus said to his disciples, "Have faith in God. I tell you the truth, you can say to this mountain, 'May you be lifted up and thrown into the sea,' and it will happen. But you must really believe it will happen and have no doubt in your heart. I tell you, you can pray for anything, and if you believe that you've received it, it will be yours. But when you are praying, first forgive anyone you are holding a grudge against, so that your Father in heaven will forgive your sins, too." (Mark 11:22-25 NLT)

Earlier in this passage, Jesus uses the example of a leafy but fruitless fig tree to illustrate the uselessness of a big, beautiful temple that draws people to itself but no one to God. Now he turns the metaphor of the fig tree into a lesson about discipleship.

To be effective disciples, Jesus says, we must be sure of our faith and confident in our prayers to God. Without God's help, we cannot cultivate the precious fruit that draws people, not to our good deeds but to the goodness of God. It is the Spirit's work to transform us from leafy ornamentals into productive trees that can nourish hungry souls and heal broken relationships.

Jesus goes on to name two fleshly characteristics that block our prayers and keep us from producing this nourishing fruit: unbelief and unforgiveness.

Although we may believe in God, our **unbelief** limits the effectiveness of our prayers. We may pray guardedly, holding back areas of our lives where we don't trust God to be sovereign—over our finances, our future, our ambitions, our relationships. Perhaps we doubt God's goodness or trustworthiness because we've suffered through a painful circumstance, and God did not rescue us. We deny the Spirit room enough in our hearts to cultivate the fruit that God desires.

Jesus also warns that **unforgiveness** stands in the way of effective prayer. Why? Because grudges rival the Spirit for control of our lives and relationships. Refusing to forgive always indicates an area of our hearts that has remained dark and hidden from the light of God's grace and forgiveness. Opening ourselves to God's mercy softens our anger and gives us both reason and desire to forgive others.

Heavenly Father, when my prayers seem to go unanswered, I typically look to you for the reason why instead of looking at myself. Help me to identify those areas of my life where I struggle with unbelief and unforgiveness. I pray to be fertile ground where your Spirit can cultivate the fruit you desire for my life and my relationships. Amen

Dig Deeper: Psalm 92:12-15; Mark 9:23-24

Reflect: What issue in my life keeps me from surrendering my whole heart to God when I pray? What do I need from God to help me resolve this issue?

Thought for Today: Releasing a grudge gives the Spirit room to work in our hearts.

Saturday/Sunday

Weekend Review

Settle in: I quiet myself and acknowledge God's presence. I offer God my time and attention. I ask the Spirit to help me review my week with clarity and understanding.

Review with gratitude: I allow memories of the week to flow through me like a slow river. I notice special moments and gifts, large and small, for which I am thankful. I take some time to acknowledge these blessings before God and express my gratitude.

Celebrate: I recall what went well for me this week.

- When did I experience life-giving feelings, such as joy, peace, love, generosity, or being on a right path?
- When did I feel God's nearness?
- How did I practice new insights from my forgiveness work this week?
- In what ways did God counsel and help me this week?

Confront: I recall what did not go well for me this week.

- When did I experience life-draining feelings, such as anger, anxiety, envy, sadness, fear, rebelliousness, or being on a wrong path?
- When did God seem most distant?
- What forgiveness practices did I find difficult or impossible?
- In what ways did I resist God's counsel and help this week?

Talk it over: I talk with God about what I've discovered.

- I praise and thank God for the work of his Spirit in my life this week.
- I acknowledge areas of my life where I am resistant to God's

call and counsel.

- I ask God for the grace I need to continue this journey of forgiving and practicing God's ways in my relationships.

Close with prayer: I pray along with this Celtic nature prayer:

There is no plant in the ground

But is full of God's virtue,

There is no form in the strand

But is full of God's blessing.

Right it is to praise God.

There is no life in the sea,

There is no creature in the river,

There is nothing in the firmament,

But proclaims God's goodness.

Right it is to praise God.

There is no bird on the wing,

There is no star in the sky,

There is nothing beneath the sun,

But proclaims God's goodness.

Right it is to praise God. Amen

Week Nine

Monday

Born for Trouble

Then Eliphaz the Temanite replied to Job…"But evil does not spring from the soil, and trouble does not sprout from the earth. People are born for trouble as readily as sparks fly up from a fire." (Job 4:1; 5:6-7 NLT)

When we experience hardship, we instinctively look for a cause. If we can determine the cause-and-effect relationship responsible for our trouble, then we not only validate our understanding of how the world works but also imagine that such understanding can help us avoid the same trouble in the future.

In the above quote, Job's friend Eliphaz argues that humans are responsible for their own troubles. Job's overall story, however, teaches what Eliphaz did not seem to know, that as humans we suffer not only because of our own sin but also because we are subject to forces we cannot control or sidestep.

Because of the fall, all creation suffers decline and destruction, yet creation itself is morally neutral. It is not evil when a cheetah takes down a gazelle, or a stately oak succumbs to root rot. These are natural calamities. Humans alone, because we are made in God's image, possess a will and moral choice. Every day, even moment by moment, we choose for good or for evil, for right or for wrong, for generosity or for selfishness. Our suffering, more often than not, is a complex web of natural calamity and the interplay of our choices and the choices of others.

Eliphaz was right when he claimed that people are born for trouble. Although we want to pin the blame for our suffering on someone, perhaps ourselves, or on some circumstance we can name, such blaming is usually simplistic and fruitless. In his final discourse, Jesus tells his disciples to expect hardship as a natural part of life but not to let the hardship conquer them. Jesus promises his peace to those who live in faith, even in the midst of trouble (John 16:33).

If we can accept that trouble is an inescapable—and often inexplicable—part of life, then we can rest from blaming and resenting and retaliating. Instead, we can focus on finding God in the midst of our suffering and ask, *what does it mean to have God with me in this trouble? How will God use this trouble to make me stronger?*

Heavenly Father, I admit to having a secret belief that, if everyone acted the way they should, there would be no unhappiness in the world. Too often I find myself saying, "If it weren't for this or for that, I would be content." Help me to accept trouble as part of my journey with you toward spiritual maturity. Teach me to trust you so that I can let go of my need to blame. Amen

Dig Deeper: Psalm 119:71; John 16:33

Reflect: The next time things go wrong, instead of looking for someone to blame, I can immediately look to God for grace and perspective.

Thought for Today: Trouble will find us whether we sin or not.

Tuesday

The Supernatural Power of Unity

After Jesus said this, he looked toward heaven and prayed…"I have given them the glory that you gave me, that they may be one as we are one—I in them and you in me—so that they may be brought to complete unity. Then the world will know that you sent me and have loved them even as you have loved me." (John 17:1, 22-23 NIV)

Unity among believers is an important theme stressed repeatedly in New Testament writings. The *glory* that Jesus received from the Father and gave to his disciples is the radiant, beautiful, and powerful manifestation of God. As the Father was with the

Son, so has the Son come to us as *Immanuel*—"God with us"—and we who believe become temples to house the divine Glory that shines through our lives. Through mystical union with the Holy Spirit, the Son is in us as the Father is also in him. The same Spirit in each of us is *at the same time* in *all* believers, making us one body, unified by the Spirit, with Christ at the head.

Paul expresses this mystical unity in the passage, Ephesian 4:3-6: "Make every effort to keep the unity of the Spirit through the bond of peace. There is one body and one Spirit, just as you were called to one hope when you were called; one Lord, one faith, one baptism; one God and Father of all, who is over all and through all and in all" (NIV).

Unity among believers, then, is not a matter of getting along without quarreling, nor is it about finding common doctrine. Unity in the Church is a matter of each individual being in constant communion with the Father and the Son, and thereby being *supernaturally* connected to all other believers who are in like communion. We are unified by the glorious presence of God living simultaneously and profoundly in each and all of his children.

Heavenly Father, make me a fit temple for your Holy Spirit. Help me to recognize how I discourage unity in my church community by focusing on myself instead of on you. Remove the unholy and the unwholesome from my life so the world can see your glorious presence in me. Amen

Dig Deeper: John 1:14; 1 Corinthians 3:16-17

Reflect: How does unity among believers make God visible to the world?

Thought for Today: Faithful communion with God is the key to unity in the Church.

Week Nine

Wednesday

Tenants for God

> While Moses was on Mount Sinai, the LORD said to him…"The land must never be sold on a permanent basis, for the land belongs to me. You are only foreigners and tenant farmers working for me." (Leviticus 25:23 NLT)

When we choose to follow Christ, we voluntarily give up ownership of our lives. In our acceptance of God's new covenant in Christ, we acknowledge that we—all that we are, all that we have, and all to which we aspire—have been bought with the high price of the cross. Instead of working and planning to serve ourselves, we shift our perspective and now work for God, serving his aspirations and desires for this world.

When we choose to follow Christ, we, in effect, become tenants of our own lives and stewards of all that God has given us. He now owns everything for his own use. Of course, this was always the case. In following Christ, we merely acknowledge the truth of it.

In fact, we can think of our relationships as "land" that God has leased to us, territory he wants us to work and tend and nurture toward a harvest that serves his purpose. God assigns to us particular people and situations and then gives us resources to work them toward fruition that honors and glorifies him. Our job as tenant farmers is to submit to God's plan for this particular bit of territory and obey his instructions. God's job is to call into maturity the crop he intends.

This perspective can be especially helpful when we are facing a difficult relationship. Rather than asking ourselves, "What will serve me best?" we can ask, "What will serve God best in this situation?" Then, instead of trying to manipulate circumstances to achieve a particular outcome, we can focus all our efforts on submitting ourselves to God's wiser plan and being obedient. The crop he intends might be hidden from our understanding, but faith teaches us that if we obey God, we don't have to worry about the outcome. God will always produce good fruit in accordance with his purpose in the season that God decides.

Heavenly Father, life becomes easier when I remember that I am not the owner of my life but merely a tenant who is in very wise and capable hands. Thank you for entrusting me with so many blessings, especially the people in my life. Help me to serve you by serving them. Teach me the value of obedience in situations that are difficult and painful. Give me grace to let go of my illusions of control and to give your Spirit freedom to produce good fruit in my life and relationships. Amen

Dig Deeper: Psalm 1:3; Isaiah 27:6

Reflect: What does it mean to be a tenant of my life rather than its owner? How might this perspective shift my approach in a particular relationship?

Thought for Today: The more we yield to God, the more good fruit God will yield through us.

Thursday

My True and Upright Self

But I did find this: God created people to be virtuous, but they have each turned to follow their own downward path. (Ecclesiastes 7:29 NLT)

The above comment by King Solomon has been translated in various ways:

- "God made us plain and simple, but we have made ourselves very complicated" (GNT).
- "God made men and women true and upright; we're the ones who've made a mess of things" (MSG).
- "God made people to be good, but they have found all kinds of

ways to be bad" (NCV).

Whichever translation you prefer, the passage might sound depressing if it weren't so hopeful and reassuring.

The good news for us is, God made men and women to be *good*, true and upright, virtuous. He did not create us to be sinful and to do evil but *to do good works*. God designed us to be part of his perfect creation and fit companions for his holy and loving presence. But sin interferes. We know firsthand the terrible persuasive power of sin to twist and corrupt what God has set in place. We also know such a force is beyond anything we can control with our will alone. We need God's help to turn us away from that "downward path." We need God's strength and we need faith to believe that our lives can indeed be turned.

Thankfully, when we choose to become followers of Christ, we don't have to reinvent ourselves or learn how to change a bad person into a good one. We don't modify our sin nature to conform to a Christian exterior. Instead, we begin to discard sins like fetters that have kept us bound and crippled. Maturing in Christ means releasing the person *we have always been*, inside our souls, before sin began to twist and reshape us. As the author of Hebrews describes a runner shedding whatever holds him back in the race God has set before him, we cast off the old crippling nature until we can stand true and upright, reflections of God's image, ready for his work.

Each of us has that strong, beautiful potential already inside, waiting to be freed. The more we grow to resemble Christ, the more strongly we reveal God's original handiwork in us, that unique character and soul that he longs to restore and see perfected.

Heavenly Father, sometimes I glimpse the person you created me to be—the one who is joyful and unafraid and finely tuned to the beauty and goodness you have woven into your creation. For a moment, I feel aligned with you, but then I lose it. I forget who you made me to be, and my fears and doubts and loneliness return. Help me, Father, to feel at my core not shame and ugliness but rather the beauty of being specially crafted by you with love and care and for your good purpose. Teach me to see myself as you see me and to honor who you made me to be, not because I am so special and great but because you are. Amen

Dig Deeper: Romans 7:15; Ephesians 2:10; Hebrews 12:1-3

Reflect: When am I most likely to glimpse the shining soul God created me to be? Who encourages me to be this person?

Thought for Today: When we discard our sin, we set free our potential to be beautiful and good, as God always intended.

Friday

The Best Revenge

> If you come across your enemy's ox or donkey that has strayed away, take it back to its owner. If you see that the donkey of someone who hates you has collapsed under its load, do not walk by. Instead, stop and help. (Exodus 23:4-5 NLT)

Through the Law of Moses, God gave the Israelites an astonishing command. "When you suffer harm," God said in effect, "don't retaliate with evil. Instead, show your enemy kindness and compassion."

Jesus amplified this command when he told his disciples to *love* their enemies and *pray* for their persecutors.

This idea of answering evil with goodness is radical and countercultural in any era. As modern-day believers, we are charged with the same command and for the same reason: By loving our enemies, we show ourselves to be true children of God, and we advance God's work of bringing peace and healing to a damaged world. As God's ambassadors, we resist the urge to compete and win conflicts, but rather we do what we can to bring love and forgiveness into whatever relationships come our way.

Interestingly, God's nature becomes most visible in those very relationships that cause us the most pain and trouble. When the world expects revenge and harsh treatment but instead sees us responding to our enemies with the fruit of God's loving Spirit, then the world takes notice and God is glorified.

Heavenly Father, it is hard to be thankful for the difficult, painful relationships in my life. When I feel angry and frustrated with others, give me a strong sense of your Spirit. Take each vengeful feeling in me and transform it into fruit that benefits those who wish me harm. Help me to extend your grace to those who may not know they need it. Amen

Dig Deeper: Proverbs 25:21-22; 1 Peter 3:9

Reflect: When did someone show me kindness when I expected anger? What was my response?

Thought for Today: Kindness and compassion are never inappropriate.

Saturday/Sunday

Weekend Review

Settle in: I quiet myself and acknowledge God's presence. I offer God my time and attention. I ask the Spirit to help me review my week with clarity and understanding.

Review with gratitude: I allow memories of the week to flow through me like a slow river. I notice special moments and gifts, large and small, for which I am thankful. I take some time to acknowledge these blessings before God and express my gratitude.

Celebrate: I recall what went well for me this week.

- When did I experience life-giving feelings, such as joy, peace, love, generosity, or being on a right path?
- When did I feel God's nearness?

- How did I practice new insights from my forgiveness work this week?

- In what ways did God counsel and help me this week?

Confront: I recall what did not go well for me this week.

- When did I experience life-draining feelings, such as anger, anxiety, envy, sadness, fear, rebelliousness, or being on a wrong path?

- When did God seem most distant?

- What forgiveness practices did I find difficult or impossible?

- In what ways did I resist God's counsel and help this week?

Talk it over: I talk with God about what I've discovered.

- I praise and thank God for the work of his Spirit in my life this week.

- I acknowledge areas of my life where I am resistant to God's call and counsel.

- I ask God for the grace I need to continue this journey of forgiving and practicing God's ways in my relationships.

Close with prayer: I pray along with this prayer of John Hus (1369-1415):

Lord Jesus Christ, I commit my soul into your hands,

for you have redeemed me with your blood.

Father in Heaven, do not hold against my enemies the sins they

commit against me;

rather, let me know that they will be at peace in your presence.

O Holy Spirit, enlighten their hearts,

so that the truth of the Gospel may open their eyes,

and its praise may be spread everywhere,

forever and ever. Amen.

Week Ten

Monday

Beauty from the Ashes

For surely I know the plans I have for you, says the LORD, plans for your welfare and not for harm, to give you a future with hope. (Jeremiah 29:11 NRSV)

One of the hardest things to forgive is losing a dream or a future we've been counting on because of someone's harmful action. Perhaps a child is molested, and an unspoiled future is lost. A parent suffers estrangement from an adult son or daughter whose choices have caused friction and brokenness in the family. Criminal activity cheats a couple out of their retirement money, or a home invasion traumatizes its victim into never feeling safe again. Deception and betrayal damage a relationship beyond repair.

The Jeremiah passage quoted above was meant to encourage displaced Israelites who had lost their homeland, yet its message can encourage us as well. God reassures all his people that he is present and sovereign even in the most woeful times. When we lose a cherished dream or suffer loss that redefines our future, God says that the future still belongs to him. This means that, although a painful circumstance derailed our plans, it did not derail God's plans for us. Even from the worst damage and suffering, God can repair and restore us to be the people he intended for us to be all along. No evil force can outmaneuver God. No devastation is so final that God cannot raise beauty and wholeness from its ashes.

When a crushing loss hits us, and we have no hope of going back or recovering what was lost, we must look toward a future that is reshaped and redefined. Trusting God in such a difficult circumstance tests our faith in God's nature and power. Do we believe God is good and loving and just? Do we believe God was never absent but always present with us in our suffering? Can we trust God to lead us in our blindness and confusion to a higher place, where character is built up and the heart learns lessons of humility and gratitude, love and mercy?

Week Ten

Instead of allowing a hurtful circumstance to reshape us, we can choose to open ourselves to God's reshaping. We can trust that God will help us toward an uprightness and beauty of soul that was always in his plans for us.

Heavenly Father, I ask for more faith to trust you with my life and my future. Help me to see past my losses and hurts and believe that your love is deeper and stronger than anything our sinful world can conceive. When I feel crushed, heal and restore me to wholeness. When I lose hope, help me to rise and walk with you toward the future you have already secured for me. Amen

Dig Deeper: Genesis 45:5; 1 Thessalonians 3:12-13

Reflect: Was something taken from me that left me angry and resentful? How could God use that very loss to my spiritual advantage?

Thought for Today: What we consider loss may be just what God will use for our gain.

Tuesday

Eyes of Light

> Now when Jesus saw the crowds, he went up on the mountainside and sat down. His disciples came to him, and he began to teach them...."The eye is the lamp of the body. If your eyes are healthy, your whole body will be full of light. But if your eyes are unhealthy, your whole body will be full of darkness. If then the light within you is darkness, how great is that darkness!" (Matthew 6:1-2, 22-23 NIV)

A familiar sixteenth-century proverb tells us that "the eyes are windows to the soul." It's true: Our eyes give away clues about our moods and emotions, whether we are telling the truth or lying, or whether we are excited or bored or confused. Unless we are very good at schooling our emotions, others can read our secret thoughts through our eyes, which is why we tend to avoid meeting another's gaze when we have something to hide.

The above passage additionally teaches us that the eye not only reveals but actually *determines* our inner state. Whatever the eye takes in, Jesus says, the heart receives and retains. If we want to improve the quality of our inner being, we should examine how we perceive and interpret the world we see.

The *healthy* eye—also translated "generous" or "pure"—looks for God in the world and takes in the light of his truth. Unclouded by selfishness, greed, or bitterness, the healthy eye observes others without distortion or bias, so the image taken into the heart will be true and real and enlightening.

The *unhealthy* eye, on the other hand, is fixed on oneself. It perceives others through the dark filter of self-interest and thereby distorts what our heart receives and believes.

We can choose whether to take light or darkness into our hearts. For example, notice how your opinions and preconceived notions filter or "darken" the way you see other people. Recognize when dark emotions are clouding your perceptions and biasing you toward wrong assumptions about people's motives and behaviors. Many conflicts and misunderstandings can be avoided by simply clearing your vision.

Heavenly Father, thank you for the truth that always gives light, even when it exposes something dark or dangerous. Grant me wisdom to see others realistically and without the distortions that lead me to make false assumptions or take unwarranted offense. Give me grace to ask forgiveness from those whom I have misjudged and to rid my heart of the darkness I received through clouded vision. Amen

Dig Deeper: Psalm 51:10; Isaiah 2:5

Reflect: What recent offense might simply be a case of clouded vision?

Thought for Today: Let go of bitterness and let more light into

Week Ten

your heart.

Wednesday

Go and Love

> Then the LORD said to me, "Go and love your wife again, even though she commits adultery with another lover. This will illustrate that the LORD still loves Israel, even though the people have turned to other gods and love to worship them." (Hosea 3:1-2 NLT)

The story of Hosea and his unfaithful wife is important because God uses it to illustrate his covenant love and faithfulness to unfaithful Israel. The story also shows us how to respond in a godly way to difficult relationships of our own. When we follow Hosea's example of redemptive love and forgiveness to his wife, Gomer, we follow Christ.

Gomer had deserted her husband and three children to live a life of prostitution. Adultery and prostitution were serious crimes, and Hosea had a right not only to divorce her but to have her stoned to death as well. Instead, God commanded him to redeem her and reinstate her high position in the marriage.

We glean two important principles from Hosea's example.

First, God required love-in-action. We don't know if Hosea sat at home pining for his lost love, but God said that loving silently from afar wasn't good enough. Hosea had to put his love into practical action. "Go," God told him, "and love your wife again." It takes courage to step toward someone who has betrayed us and offer kindness. We may suffer silently and keep our love locked away for fear of being hurt again. Or we may have allowed the betrayal to turn our love bitter. God's command is to "go and love." Such an act is unnatural and requires the Spirit's help. We may need boldness and wisdom and a fresh, compassionate view of the other person to step out and offer forgiveness.

Second, Hosea's act of love required humility. The text implies that Gomer had sold herself into slavery. Even worse, she was a slave of little value because the price for her redemption was so meager. Honor was an important value in that culture, and Gomer's betrayal not only hurt Hosea personally but humiliated him publicly. We can imagine his friends arguing against the folly of his putting down good money to redeem a worthless wife. To act in love after a betrayal not only takes courage but a good dose of humility. We must be willing to lay aside our pride and reputation for the other person's sake. Gomer needed to be saved from her life of debasement, and God had positioned Hosea to redeem her. In like manner, God sometimes positions us to pay the cost of restoring someone who needs grace and a second chance.

Heavenly Father, your story of Hosea is a story about your love for me and why you sent Christ to pay the price for my betrayal. Thank you for your relentless love that would not let me continue to live in sin and debasement. Thank you that Christ was willing to be humiliated for my sake. Give me courage and humility to show love to those who have wronged me and to forgive with the same grace you have given me. Amen

Dig Deeper: Psalm 32:1; Matthew 18:21-22

Reflect: What is the price I might pay in forgiving someone who betrayed me?

Thought for Today: Forgiveness must be acted out in love, or it's just words.

Thursday

How to Get Even

Don't testify against your neighbors without cause; don't lie about them. And don't say, "Now I can pay them back for what they've done to me! I'll get even with them!" (Proverbs 24:28-29 NLT)

Week Ten

Thirst for revenge is a natural instinct. Everyone knows that nasty little spirit who whispers, "You don't have to take that insult lying down—get even!" Consequently, there is no stronger witness for our faith than responding well to a personal injury or offense.

Life repeatedly presents us with opportunities to choose God's way or the way of the world. We can demand an eye for an eye, Jesus says, or we can choose to treat our neighbors with the same generosity and forgiveness that we would hope to receive from them. Peter further contrasts God's way to the world's way of revenge: "Don't repay evil for evil. Don't retaliate with insults when people insult you. Instead, pay them back with a blessing. That is what God has called you to do, and he will bless you for it" (1 Peter 3:9 NLT).

Revenge may seem a sweet solution, but it rapidly turns to poison. The world's way of "getting even" means conforming our minds and behaviors to the level of hurt and meanness that we have received. Even subtle forms of payback, such as passive-aggressive behaviors or withdrawal of simple courtesies, lower us into the mud and weaken our faith walk with God. We lose our sense of *holiness*—our identity of being set apart for God—as we become indistinguishable from the unbelieving world.

In contrast, God's way of "getting even" is to align our minds and behaviors as evenly as possible with those of Christ Jesus. The Spirit resets our priorities to match God's desire for the situation. Instead of lowering ourselves into the mud, the apostle Paul tells us to "set your hearts on things above, where Christ is seated at the right hand of God" (Colossians 3:2 NIV). Consequently, we can offer prayer instead of payback and kindness instead of criticism. As the rich recipients of God's blessing and forgiveness, we can offer the same to those who have hurt and insulted us.

Heavenly Father, I admit I am quick to judge and condemn those who offend me. Even worse, I have lashed out in my anger and tried to hurt back in the same ways that I have been hurt. Forgive me for missing so many opportunities to respond with kindness and forgiveness to the world's cruelty and thereby be your witness for good. Thank you for your mercy and for your patient instruction in better ways to handle relationship difficulties. Amen

Dig Deeper: Luke 6:27-31; Romans 8:5; 12:2, 19-21

Reflect: How might God bless me when I choose to bless my offender?

Thought for Today: Payback only puts us in debt alongside our debtor.

Friday

Piety That Counts

Then he began to speak, and taught them, saying…"Beware of practicing your piety before others in order to be seen by them; for then you have no reward from your Father in heaven." (Matthew 5:2; 6:1 NRSV)

How do you "practice your piety"? In these verses and the ones that follow, Jesus names almsgiving, praying, and fasting as practices that show religious devotion. In our day, we might add studying the Bible, listening to Christian music, or serving meals to the homeless. We attend church faithfully and donate turkeys and canned goods and clothing for distribution to the needy at Thanksgiving and Christmas.

All these practices are good, Jesus would say, but *beware*. Godly deeds can easily mask a heart that is secretly far from God. Look at the rewards you receive for your good deeds, and you will discover the secret desire that motivates your piety.

Jesus divides these rewards into two categories: *being seen by others* and *seeing God*.

Being seen by others. The *hypocrites* (literally, "actors") pretend devotion to God when they are really devoted to attracting praise and attention. We don't have to announce our religious devotion on street corners to qualify as hypocrites. Piety becomes fake any time we perform good deeds with the goal of being seen as a good person, whether in the eyes of others or in our own opinion. The reward of being admired can feel so good that our practicing piety can become compulsive and addictive. Jesus warns that ego strokes are all the satisfaction hypocrites can expect to receive.

Seeing God. Earlier in his teaching, Jesus tells his disciples, "Blessed are the pure in heart, for they will see God" (Matthew 5:8 NRSV). For those who seek God with pure motives, God's reward is Himself. Jesus challenges us to take the focus off ourselves and our need for attention and instead to give praise and attention to God. Then all our piety practices—praying, Bible reading, worshipping, serving others—become opportunities to find and be with God instead of platforms for promoting ourselves. We love, forgive, and serve one another, not so we can credit ourselves with goodness but because these are attributes of the God we desire and the qualities that bring us close to him.

Heavenly Father, you know my heart better than I do. You know my secret desires. Show me in what ways I am an actor rather than a true follower of you. Change my heart to desire you more than I desire the admiration of others and my own good opinion of myself. Amen

Dig Deeper: Psalm 37:4; Matthew 5:8

Reflect: When I list the rewards I seek for my good deeds, is seeing God among them?

Thought for Today: Our good deeds matter most when they help us see God.

Saturday/Sunday

Weekend Review

Settle in: I quiet myself and acknowledge God's presence. I offer

God my time and attention. I ask the Spirit to help me review my week with clarity and understanding.

Review with gratitude: I allow memories of the week to flow through me like a slow river. I notice special moments and gifts, large and small, for which I am thankful. I take some time to acknowledge these blessings before God and express my gratitude.

Celebrate: I recall what went well for me this week.

- When did I experience life-giving feelings, such as joy, peace, love, generosity, or being on a right path?
- When did I feel God's nearness?
- How did I practice new insights from my forgiveness work this week?
- In what ways did God counsel and help me this week?

Confront: I recall what did not go well for me this week.

- When did I experience life-draining feelings, such as anger, anxiety, envy, sadness, fear, rebelliousness, or being on a wrong path?
- When did God seem most distant?
- What forgiveness practices did I find difficult or impossible?
- In what ways did I resist God's counsel and help this week?

Talk it over: I talk with God about what I've discovered.

- I praise and thank God for the work of his Spirit in my life this week.
- I acknowledge areas of my life where I am resistant to God's call and counsel.
- I ask God for the grace I need to continue this journey of forgiving and practicing God's ways in my relationships.

Close with prayer: I pray along with this prayer of Martin Bucer

Week Ten

(1491-1551):

> *Merciful God and Father,*
>
> *draw my heart and soul to your Son,*
>
> *so that I may receive such a love as his with living faith and eternal gratitude,*
>
> *and therefore die to all evil more and more each day,*
>
> *grow and increase in all goodness,*
>
> *and lead my life with respect, patience, and love toward my neighbor.*
>
> *Greatly comforted by your holy gospel,*
>
> *I will now and always call upon you, my God and Father. Amen.*

Week Eleven

Monday

Fudging the Facts

> The chief priests and the whole Sanhedrin were looking for false evidence against Jesus so that they could put him to death. But they did not find any, though many false witnesses came forward. Finally two came forward and declared, "This fellow said, 'I am able to destroy the temple of God and rebuild it in three days.'" Then the high priest stood up and said to Jesus, "Are you not going to answer? What is this testimony that these men are bringing against you?" But Jesus remained silent. (Matthew 26:59-63a NIV)

Jesus' trial was rigged from the start. The religious leaders weren't looking for truth and justice but for lies damaging enough to warrant a petition to the Roman governor for Jesus' execution. They found their answer in two witnesses who came forward and testified about what they heard Jesus say. We know their testimony was an inaccurate quote of what the Gospel of John records in 2:19, where Jesus claims that if the temple were destroyed, he would raise it again in three days. Scripture goes on to say that the "temple" Jesus spoke of was his own body.

So, were these witnesses lying or telling the truth as they saw it? Were they collaborators or mere pawns in the religious conspiracy to destroy Jesus? The fact is, we don't know.

We do know that eye-witness testimony can be unreliable because we are humans and not digital recorders. We cannot take in every detail of a situation but filter what goes into our brains. Moreover, every time we take out a memory to share it with others, we report our *interpretation* of what we heard or saw, tweaking facts and leaving out details in a process that is mostly unconscious.

This inaccurate reporting gets worse when we have an agenda we want our testimony to support. Perhaps we are discussing a political candidate or arguing a doctrinal issue. We may be called to testify about a loved one who has gotten into trouble with the law. We may want to boost our reputation, save our job, or avoid conflict in a fragile relationship. Consequently, we may speak in half-truths, fudging the facts and glossing over details because we want our testimony to sway others toward the outcome we desire.

Although we may not intend to lie or exaggerate, we can fall into such behaviors without conscious thought. With some effort, however, we can teach ourselves to recognize when we are fabricating information about ourselves and others, even incrementally, and practice speaking only the truth.

Heavenly Father, help me to notice the inaccuracies in the stories I tell others. Forgive me for deliberately misinforming people or telling half-truths in attempts to further my own interests. I know that all lying is abhorrent to you and contrary to your nature. Teach me to love truth and to guard my spoken words. Amen

Dig Deeper: John 8:44-45; Colossians 3:9-10

Reflect: In what areas of my life am I most likely to exaggerate or otherwise speak falsely? What steps can I take to correct this habit?

Thought for Today: The smallest lie causes ripples that can never be recovered.

Tuesday

Forgiver's Prayer

> Moses bowed to the ground at once and worshiped. "Lord," he said, "if I have found favor in your eyes, then let the Lord go with us. Although this is a stiff-necked people, forgive our wickedness and our sin, and take us as your inheritance." (Exodus 34:8-9 NIV)

This prayer follows on the heels of Moses' coming down from the mountain with a freshly minted Ten Commandments, only to find the people worshipping a golden calf. In his anger, Moses smashes the stone tablets and orders punishment for the idol worshippers. Yet now he returns to God's presence to beg forgiveness on behalf of the people.

Although their action betrayed Moses as their leader, Moses did not take personal offense. Instead, his anger was on behalf of both the God he loved and the people he loved, who now bore the weight of terrible sin and would suffer for it. Notice also that Moses asks the Lord's forgiveness for "our" sin and wickedness. He had no part in worshipping the idol, yet he includes himself among the unclean who need God's restoration. He identifies more with a disobedient people than with a holy and perfect Judge.

Moses' plea on behalf of the Israelites is a good example of the intercessory effort that Jesus describes when he tells his disciples to bless and pray for their enemies. A prayer on behalf of our enemies today might read something like this: *Holy God and sovereign Lord, I put before you [offender's name], whose wrongful action has grieved your Spirit and violated your law of love. In the name of Jesus, I ask your forgiveness. You are a just God, yet we seek your mercy because we are weak and prone to sin and selfish actions. Because of your steadfast love, I ask you to cover me and cover [offender's name] with the righteousness of Jesus, that we may not suffer the punishment we deserve.*

If we cannot pray these words from a sincere heart, then we know we still have forgiveness work to do.

Heavenly Father, when someone hurts or offends me, I typically assume your role as righteous and holy Judge. I pray for humility like Moses' to recognize that I am like the person who hurt me, and I need your love and mercy just as much. Soften my heart until I desire only blessing and restoration for those who wrong me. Amen

Dig Deeper: Luke 6:28; Acts 7:59-60

Reflect: In what ways can I admit that I am like my offender?

Week Eleven

Thought for Today: Forgiveness is not complete until we can pray for blessing on our enemy.

Wednesday

Asset or Stumbling Block?

From that time on, Jesus began to show his disciples that he must go to Jerusalem and undergo great suffering at the hands of the elders and chief priests and scribes, and be killed, and on the third day be raised. And Peter took him aside and began to rebuke him, saying, "God forbid it, Lord! This must never happen to you." But he turned and said to Peter, "Get behind me, Satan! You are a stumbling block to me; for you are setting your mind not on divine things but on human things." (Matthew 16:21-23 NRSV)

At first glance, Jesus' rebuke seems unfair. Peter expresses concern for the Master he loves, and instead of being grateful, Jesus criticizes and insults him. Why so harsh?

Although Peter has just declared Jesus to be the Messiah and the Son of the living God, he does not yet understand what that means. Jesus is fully God, yet he is also fully human, a mystery that Satan fully understood when he tempted Jesus to throw himself down from the top of the temple in Jerusalem (Luke 4:9). Satan was implying, "You are too special to suffer like an ordinary human." Jesus rejected the offer and rebuked Satan for testing God's commitment to saving creation through his own painful death on a cross.

Now Peter unwittingly echoes Satan's temptation, and Jesus rejects it with the same fervor. Moreover, Jesus is driving home a lesson for all the disciples, including we modern-day followers. Jesus warns us all to look beyond our natural human vision and embrace God's bigger plan. We must look for God's perspective in all our daily concerns so that we can be assets rather than stumbling blocks to the kingdom God wants to build in our midst.

We serve God best when we "set our minds" on divine things. This means taking time to study God's word and imagine what God wants and expects from us as we deal with life. It means learning to deal with people in ways that serve God's redemptive purpose rather than through habits that serve our own purposes.

We might ask ourselves these mind-setting questions:

- What does God see in this person that I, with my human eyesight, have difficulty seeing?
- How might trusting God's sovereignty change my attitude toward a troublesome person or a painful circumstance?
- In what ways have I set my mind on human things and made myself a stumbling block to building God's kingdom in my family, my workplace, my community, or my church?

Heavenly Father, I ask for spiritual sensitivity to notice your presence and purpose in every aspect of my life. May knowing you as my Lord fundamentally change my approach to every person and every relationship, that I may be an asset rather than a stumbling block to your good plans. Amen

Dig Deeper: Matthew 4:5-7; 16:15-19; 2 Corinthians 5:16

Reflect: How does a human mindset contribute to conflict? How might a divine perspective change my behavior?

Thought for Today: Holding a grudge makes you a stumbling block to God's good plans.

Thursday

How to Deflect Cruel Words

Come near and rescue me; deliver me because of my foes. You know how I am scorned, disgraced and shamed; all my enemies are before you. Scorn has broken my heart and has left me helpless; I looked for sympathy, but there was none, for comforters, but I found none. (Psalm 69:18-20 NIV)

The old adage, "sticks and stones may break my bones, but names will never hurt me," is a lie.

David wrote that *his heart was broken* by the cruel things being said about him. We all know what it feels like to be falsely accused or criticized, to be mocked for a mistake or a personal flaw, or to be the target of an ugly rumor. Typical reactions to such cruelties are to feel anger, shame, defensiveness, and especially helplessness—once spoken, words are difficult to combat or control. Regardless of their veracity, rumors tend to spread like wildfire, scorching reputations and ruining relationships.

Cruel words are especially devastating when they come from the mouth of a trusted friend or loved one. *Betrayal* adds a layer of pain to any verbal injury. David's "enemies" might well have included those closest to him, those whom he loved and trusted and who, by the same token, could hurt him most deeply.

David's psalm shows us by example how to deal with ugly words and vicious rumors. He brought his heart full of pain to God and asked him for rescue. Offering our hearts to God gives God the opportunity to shift our perspective and keep us from despairing. Like David, instead of reliving the sting of hateful words, we can reflect on the beauty and faithfulness of our Father who cares for us: "Answer me, LORD, out of the goodness of your love; in your great mercy turn to me. Do not hide your face from your servant; answer me quickly, for I am in trouble." (Psalm 69:16-17 NIV).

Heavenly Father, sometimes I catch myself ruminating on someone's cruel words and reliving the pain of them. I know it's useless to hang onto such words, which I can never erase or change by wishing them different. At such times, please rescue me by reminding me how precious I am to you and how faithful and merciful and loving you have always been to me. Protect my spirit from the lies wrapped in cruel taunts and accusations. If you see any truth in these words, please show me gently and help me to repent of whatever there is in me that needs changing. Amen

Dig Deeper: Psalm 42:9-11; Matthew 27:27-31, 38-44

Reflect: What stinging words still haunt me? I can write them down and ask God to release me from their power.

Thought for Today: Harsh words are the sticks and stones that break our hearts.

Friday

No Room for Idols

You can be sure that no immoral, impure, or greedy person will inherit the Kingdom of Christ and of God. For a greedy person is an idolater, worshiping the things of this world. (Ephesians 5:5 NLT)

The apostle Paul makes it plain that idolaters have no place in God's kingdom. Why? Because idolaters pledge their hearts and actions to something or someone other than God.

Our cravings for the things of this world can consume us, turning us deaf to the counsel of the Spirit, stealing our attention and worship away from God, and discouraging us from following Christ.

When we refuse to forgive, we choose the path of the greedy idolater. Our pain and outrage loom larger than our desire to please God.

We harden our hearts and hold out for satisfaction. Paul says, in effect, that clinging to our grudges makes us idolaters and unfit for Christ's kingdom.

Take a look at the list below and see if you can identify which idols are stealing your heart away from God.

Ten Idols of the Unforgiver:

- Expectations – I have a fixed idea of how people are supposed to treat me.

- Anger – My righteous anger keeps me strong and safe from further injury.

- Reputation – I fear what people will think of me if I let this offender off the hook.

- Pride – I can boast that I am a better person than the one who hurt me.

- Free Pass – Being wronged gives me a good excuse to behave badly.

- Identity – I enjoy being a victim and garnering sympathy from others.

- Power – I keep the upper hand by withholding forgiveness from my offender.

- Gossip – I relish telling others how this person wronged me.

- Safety – If I forgive, this person might hurt me again.

- Rights – I deserve to be treated better. I deserve an apology before I will forgive.

Notice how each rationalization for refusing to forgive turns us away from God and the ways of Christ's kingdom. You can add to the list by asking yourself, *what is the one thing that I cannot give up in order to follow God and forgive?* That is your idol.

Heavenly Father, I long to be fit for your kingdom. Examine my heart and show me the idols that keep me from following Christ's example and forgiving those who offend me. Give me the desire to honor and worship you above every temptation of this world. Amen

Dig Deeper: Jonah 2:8; 1 Corinthians 10:14

Reflect: How might clinging to a grudge make me unfit for Christ's kingdom?

Thought for Today: We can choose a life filled with grudges or grace.

Saturday/Sunday

Weekend Review

Settle in: I quiet myself and acknowledge God's presence. I offer God my time and attention. I ask the Spirit to help me review my week with clarity and understanding.

Review with gratitude: I allow memories of the week to flow through me like a slow river. I notice special moments and gifts, large and small, for which I am thankful. I take some time to acknowledge these blessings before God and express my gratitude.

Celebrate: I recall what went well for me this week.

- When did I experience life-giving feelings, such as joy, peace, love, generosity, or being on a right path?
- When did I feel God's nearness?
- How did I practice new insights from my forgiveness work this week?
- In what ways did God counsel and help me this week?

Confront: I recall what did not go well for me this week.

- When did I experience life-draining feelings, such as anger, anxiety, envy, sadness, fear, rebelliousness, or being on a wrong path?
- When did God seem most distant?
- What forgiveness practices did I find difficult or impossible?
- In what ways did I resist God's counsel and help this week?

Talk it over: I talk with God about what I've discovered.

- I praise and thank God for the work of his Spirit in my life this week.
- I acknowledge areas of my life where I am resistant to God's call and counsel.
- I ask God for the grace I need to continue this journey of forgiving and practicing God's ways in my relationships.

Close with prayer: I pray along with this prayer by Hartley Coleridge (1796-1849):

Be not afraid to pray—

to pray is right.

Pray, if thou canst, with hope;

But ever pray,

Though hope be weak

or sick with long delay;

Pray in the darkness, Amen

Week Twelve

Monday

Love Without Pause

O LORD, you have examined my heart and know everything about me. You know when I sit down or stand up. You know my thoughts even when I'm far away. You see me when I travel and when I rest at home. You know everything I do. You know what I am going to say even before I say it, LORD. You go before me and follow me. You place your hand of blessing on my head. Such knowledge is too wonderful for me, too great for me to understand! (Psalm 139:1-6 NLT)

One key verb unlocks the first six verses of this beautiful psalm: *know*. Lord, you *know* everything about me.

More than a simple understanding, God's *knowing* of the psalmist is the very same verb used in Genesis 4:1 to describe Adam's sexual knowing of his wife, Eve. The psalmist feels naked and vulnerable under the intensity of God's attention. He proceeds to describe all the ways that God knows him, from external activities to his innermost thoughts. God knows him so well that even the psalmist's words are anticipated before he utters them. *Such knowledge of me,* the psalmist concludes, *is beyond my comprehension. I cannot begin to fathom how thoroughly and perfectly you know and understand me.*

This realization disturbs him.

Tension runs through the rest of the psalm. The psalmist is torn between a desire to rest in the comfort of God's attention and the need to run away and hide from such intense intimacy.

We experience this same tension in our human relationships. We long for the joy of being known but fear being known too well. Our need to know and to be known is God's design for us, but fearing such intimacy is the result of our living in a fallen world. People we trust betray us; painful experiences make us cautious and unwilling to risk further pain. We feel shame over our sin and keep parts of ourselves hidden. We may lie or leave a relationship altogether to avoid exposing our guilty secrets.

Despite his resistance, the psalmist believes he is safe with God because God's gaze upon him is always loving. God surrounds him in every way, leaving him no way of escape, yet this Creator of the universe lays his hand ("palm") on the psalmist's head—a tender, intimate act at once claiming this child and reassuring him of continued welcome no matter what the almighty gaze might uncover. There is no pause in God's love, no hesitation over a weakness discovered, no withdrawal of affection to punish or condemn.

The apostle John writes that the more we live in God, the more perfect our love becomes, and perfect love casts out fear. As we follow Jesus, God perfects our love so that we can become safe havens for others who need to trust us with their naked vulnerabilities.

Heavenly Father, I understand very well the psalmist's ambivalence over submitting to your all-encompassing gaze. Thank you for your steadfast love that reassures me and helps me to offer up all my hidden corners to your compassionate and cleansing light. As you reshape my heart to resemble the heart of Jesus, teach me how to love without pause despite the sin and guilty secrets I may discover in my human relationships. Amen

Dig Deeper: Hebrews 4:12-13; 1 John 4:16-18

Reflect: How comfortable am I with the knowing gaze of God upon me?

Thought for Today: We can bear God's intimacy if we believe his love for us cannot be shaken by our sin.

Tuesday

Treasures of a Good Heart

Jesus knew their thoughts and replied... "A good person

produces good things from the treasury of a good heart, and an evil person produces evil things from the treasury of an evil heart." (Matthew 12:25, 35 NLT)

In this passage, Jesus is confronting the hypocrisy of the religious leaders, who claimed to represent God yet refused to acknowledge the divinity and authority of God's Son. They were trying to discredit Jesus by accusing him of being in league with the devil. Jesus, however, turns the tables on them and accuses them of the same thing. He points to their deceitful ways as evidence that their evil hearts did not belong to God.

A good heart, Jesus says, collects and stores what is good and precious to God. A heart full of such holy treasure generates conversations and behaviors that honor God and promote healthy relationships. Scripture lists some of these precious treasures of a good heart:

- God's wisdom (Proverbs 8:21)
- God's Word (Psalm 119:11; Job 23:12)
- God's light (John 3:19; 2 Corinthians 4:7)
- God's truth (2 Timothy 1:14)
- Fear of the Lord (Isaiah 33:6)
- Faith in God through Jesus Christ (2 Peter 1:1)
- God's promises (2 Peter 1:4)
- The Spirit's gifts - love, joy, peace, patience, kindness, goodness, faithfulness, gentleness, self-control (Galatians 5:22-23)

An evil heart, on the other hand, opposes God and rejects what is precious to God. Subject to sin's influence, an evil heart generates conflict and hurt from the "treasure" it stores up—anger, jealousy, resentment, deceit, greed, immorality, lust, idolatry, selfish ambition, arrogance, envy.

Sadly, as much as we want to follow God, we struggle with hearts that are a composite of good and evil. Paul describes our dilemma when he complains, "Although I want to do good, evil is right there with me" (Romans 7:21 NIV). We say and do things we know are hurtful to others, and later we wonder, *where did that come from? That's not how I want to act. That's not who I want to be.*

With God's help, we can take inventory of our heart's treasury and identify what does not belong. It will take effort, but we can begin to cast out the evil treasures and make room for what is truly precious and fruitful for God's kingdom.

Heavenly Father, I confess that my heart is not altogether devoted to you. I sometimes feel divided between living out the good you have deposited in me and selfishly grabbing what serves the darker corners of my desire. I ask you now to help me examine my heart and cast out the evil treasures I have collected and cherished. Amen

Dig Deeper: Matthew 3:8; Romans 7:21-25

Reflect: What is one "treasure" in my heart that God would have me cast out?

Thought for Today: Haughty and resentful attitudes reveal a heart that stores up evil treasures.

Wednesday

Stinging Arrows

Hosea put it well: I'll call nobodies and make them somebodies; I'll call the unloved and make them beloved. In the place where they yelled out, "You're nobody!" they're calling you "God's living children."

Isaiah maintained the same emphasis: If each grain of sand on the seashore were numbered and the sum labeled "chosen of God," they'd be numbers still, not names; salvation comes by personal selection. God doesn't count us; he calls us by name. Arithmetic is not his focus. (Romans 9:25-28 MSG)

God's love for you is personal. If you've been rejected and disowned by someone who was supposed to love and care for you, then this passage is God's Word for you.

Many of us have been lied to about our worth. We've been told that we are faulty, damaged, and unlovable. We've been shamed and cursed and abused. We've been labeled with ugly, hurtful names, and those stinging arrows still lodge in our hearts, causing us pain.

The God who created us, however, the One who knew our true and beautiful names from the beginning of time, dislodges the arrows by showing us the truth and inviting us to be his own children. To our Father, we are not disgusting but precious and beloved, the apple of his eye and a sweet aroma that brings him constant delight.

God paid the highest price to lift us above our hurtful human relationships and set our feet on the path that leads to an everlasting home with him. Let God show you the beautiful truth about who you really are. Receive his love and comfort, and let him bind the tender wounds inflicted by those stinging arrows you did not deserve.

Heavenly Father, I am wounded. Harsh words, contemptuous actions, violations of different sorts have pierced me deeply, and I cannot escape them. Their poison seeps into my life, tainting my happiness and robbing me of peace. Help me, Lord, to remove the arrows and the lies that shame and cripple me. Teach me how to be the person you created me to be and give me faith to trust in your love for me. Shield me, I pray, from those who wish me harm. Amen

Dig Deeper: Deuteronomy 32:10; 2 Corinthians 2:15; Ephesians 2:19

Reflect: How would I name the arrows that cause me pain?

Thought for Today: God's love is stronger and deeper than our deepest wounds.

Thursday

Living in Light

In the beginning the Word already existed. The Word was with God, and the Word was God. He existed in the beginning with God. God created everything through him, and nothing was created except through him. The Word gave life to everything that was created, and his life brought light to everyone. The light shines in the darkness, and the darkness can never extinguish it. (John 1:1-5 NLT)

Word. Life. Light. Like a good novelist, John opens his Gospel with images of his main character. Jesus is the *Word*, the very essence of almighty God made flesh to walk the earth as one of us. Jesus is eternal *life*, the very breath that animates and sustains all creation. And for humans in particular, Jesus is *light*, the means by which we can live in fellowship with God and participate in God's kingdom on earth.

This divine light lives in us in the form of the Holy Spirit when we choose to follow Christ. The Spirit illuminates us with understanding of God's ways and empowers us to overcome evil. Living the Christian life, then, means walking in the light that God provides, with eyes wide open to recognize and resist evil, and with mind and heart tuned in to what God desires for us. When we carry this divine light—this understanding of God's ways and the power to resist evil—into our relationships, supernatural things can happen.

Christ's light helps us to see people as God sees them. As we understand ourselves to be beloved children of God, we begin to recognize that every person, even our adversary, is beloved and precious to God. When God's light exposes our sin and we feel shame and sorrow over it, we realize that we have fallen as far from God as the worst criminal and are equally dependent on God's saving mercy. When we receive God's forgiveness and feel the relief of having the burden of guilt lifted from our hearts, the light within us empowers us to love and forgive those who have harmed us, and to genuinely wish them well.

Walking in the light helps us to resist the darkness that seeps into relationships and drives people apart: resentment, jealousy, deception, cruelty, pride, envy, criticism, and need to control. Opening our relationships to God's light changes the way we see and treat one another. Jesus—*Word, life,* and *light*—brought God's kingdom into our midst. When we bring Jesus into our relationships, we extend God's reign a little deeper into our world and disable the darkness that causes conflict and pain.

Heavenly Father, thank you for your light that shows me the difference between the path of sin and the path that leads to you. Open my eyes to the blind spots in my relationships, where selfish desires still control me and hurt others. Expose my prejudice and help me to value every person as a beloved child, precious to you. Empower me with the love and forgiveness I need to shine your light in every circumstance. Amen

Dig Deeper: Isaiah 50:11; Ephesians 5:8; 1 John 1:7

Reflect: What patch of darkness in my life do I need God's power to overcome?

Thought for Today: Living in God's light changes the way we see and treat one another.

Friday

Sing a New Song

O sing to the LORD a new song; sing to the LORD, all the earth. Sing to the LORD, bless his name; tell of his salvation from day to day. (Psalm 96:1-2 NRSV)

Everyone faces make-or-break situations. Something or someone comes along and hits us so hard that we either crumble or find the strength to grow and change through the adversity.

Factors that determine whether we will grow or crumble can be age and temperament, the support of peers, physical and emotional health, skills we have acquired for coping with disappointments and injustices, and the stability of our self-image. A critical factor is whether we have an enduring hope that helps us see a future beyond our current circumstance.

For those of us who belong to Christ, challenging circumstances offer the chance for God to recreate us into an image more closely aligned with God's divine mind and heart. In Christ, we find strength and hope to grow beyond our sorrow, disappointment, and pain.

Depending on the nature and depth of our adversity, the process of growing may be lengthy and arduous. It may even take years before we can look back and see the faithful hand of God holding us up and remolding our hearts, repairing the fractures and restoring our faith.

Like the psalmist, we can then sing a new song because we have arrived at a different place—in our life, in our identity, in our understanding of God. The story we tell will now incorporate this new knowledge and confidence in God, whose name we bless with new words of intimacy and gratitude. All the earth waits for us to share our story of God's saving grace. All the earth benefits when we add our unique notes to creation's ongoing hymn of praise.

Heavenly Father, there have been circumstances in my life so crushing that I did not think I could bear them. Thank you for seeking after me when I've turned away, for healing what I thought could never be healed, and for showing me a future beyond my pain. May I sing your praise with a new heart of thanksgiving and love for all the wonders of your gracious care. Amen

Dig Deeper: Isaiah 12:2; Revelation 1:5b-6

Reflect: I will write a song—a sentence, a paragraph, or a page—to reflect how God saw me through a difficult circumstance.

Thought for Today: God recreates us through our difficult circumstances.

Saturday/Sunday

Weekend Review

Settle in: I quiet myself and acknowledge God's presence. I offer God my time and attention. I ask the Spirit to help me review my week with clarity and understanding.

Review with gratitude: I allow memories of the week to flow through me like a slow river. I notice special moments and gifts, large and small, for which I am thankful. I take some time to acknowledge these blessings before God and express my gratitude.

Celebrate: I recall what went well for me this week.

- When did I experience life-giving feelings, such as joy, peace, love, generosity, or being on a right path?
- When did I feel God's nearness?
- How did I practice new insights from my forgiveness work this week?
- In what ways did God counsel and help me this week?

Confront: I recall what did not go well for me this week.

- When did I experience life-draining feelings, such as anger, anxiety, envy, sadness, fear, rebelliousness, or being on a wrong path?
- When did God seem most distant?
- What forgiveness practices did I find difficult or impossible?
- In what ways did I resist God's counsel and help this week?

Talk it over: I talk with God about what I've discovered.

- I praise and thank God for the work of his Spirit in my life this week.
- acknowledge areas of my life where I am resistant to God's call and counsel.
- I ask God for the grace I need to continue this journey of forgiving and practicing God's ways in my relationships.

Close with prayer: I pray along with this prayer of Martin Luther (1483-1546):

O Father of all mercy and God of all comfort,

strengthen and uphold me by your Spirit.

You command that I should wait on you

until the reason for my trial shall appear.

For you take no pleasure in permitting me to suffer and be grieved.

In fact, you do not permit any evil to be done

unless you can make it serve a good purpose.

You see my distress and weakness.

Therefore you will help and deliver me. Amen

A Blessing as You Go Out

Go forth now,

in the Faith which overcomes the world,

in the Hope which will not disappoint you,

in the Love which never fails.

You are ambassadors of Christ

and He is with you always.

Grace, mercy and peace,

from Father, Son and Holy Spirit,

bless, preserve and protect you all this day

and forever.

—by Ian Cowie

About the Author

Judith Ingram earned her master's degree in counseling and a certificate in biblical studies from Cornerstone Bible Academy, and studied two years at Fuller Theological Seminary. Nine years in therapy recovering from childhood abuse issues inspired her interest in speaking and writing about forgiveness. She is the author of *A Devotional Walk with Forgiveness* (2011), a time-travel fiction trilogy *Moonseed* (2013, 2014, 2015), and has contributed to the anthologies *Inspire Forgiveness* (2015), *Inspire Kindness* (2018), and *The Literary Review* (2018). She posts weekly devotionals on her blog and lives with her husband in the San Francisco East Bay Area.

www.ingramcontent.com/pod-product-compliance
Lightning Source LLC
Chambersburg PA
CBHW061658040426
42446CB00010B/1801